Awakening the True Self

Rachel

Awakening the True Self

Jacqueline Iris Daly

you are a blessing –
always know that.
love & light –
Jacqueline
x

ATHENA PRESS
LONDON

Awakening the True Self

Cover design by Melanie Lloyd

ISBN 978 1 84748 361 4

First published 2009 by
ATHENA PRESS
Queen's House, 2 Holly Road
Twickenham TW1 4EG
United Kingdom

Printed for Athena Press

It is with sincere gratitude that I dedicate this book to Alaister Whiskers, who through walking his talk inspired me to walk mine with regards to publishing the book I had within me. It was a privilege to know and study with Alaister at Ruskin College, Oxford, during the academic year 2002/2003. Although he was working with his own challenge of cancer, he never once gave me less than his undivided attention on the subject of writing and becoming a published author. Even when I thought I might have taken a wrong turn, he always found the right words to inspire, encourage and empower me. I have no doubt that the angels are now wearing an interesting line in jumpers thanks to his joining their throng.

Bless you, Alaister

With the exception of well-known people and places, no other person who has shared the journey with me has been named. This is intentional on my part. As I explain further in the book, this story is written from the place of I. I take full responsibility for the illusion I created around myself and for that reason I have chosen not to name anyone else who has been close to me. I accept totally that anyone who has shared all or part of the journey with me may have a different illusion to offer up and my offering in no way refutes theirs.

Acknowledgements

I acknowledge with joy and gratitude all those souls who have touched my life in so many ways. As with those in my book, I do not intend to name them, yet I know they will know who they are.

I will, however, particularly thank my two sons for sharing their beauty with me. I thank Source for being my constant companion and primary relationship and for guiding me so graciously to a place where I learnt to love myself and connect with joy and peace. From here I am now able to form healing relationships with others.

I'm grateful to those souls who chose to take on the challenging task of being my Karmic Angels, and I bless them twice for my healing. I also bless my friends and family who have continually supported me in being me.

I also acknowledge myself for turning up for this adventure and in so doing turning up for God.

Namaste,

Jacqueline

Contents

Introduction

THIS IS THE STORY OF A SOUL'S JOURNEY. IT'S A STORY OF courage, love and transformation, and it has a happy ending. So in some ways it could be likened to your favourite novel or film, yet it also seems a very ordinary story about a very ordinary person who has a dream about peace. Not just peace between people and nations, but between all beings, including animals and our environment. It's a big dream and it starts with finding the peace within.

As well as being an interesting story (who doesn't like reading about the lives of other people?), it also has the potential to be a spiritual 'tool kit'. I'm not suggesting you have to be of a particular faith or even have a faith for these tools to be useful to you. I'm merely inviting you to explore the opportunity for getting to know your true self and celebrating exactly who you are right now through experimenting with these tools. It isn't a case of reinventing ourselves. It's more often a case of reframing how we see ourselves and our journey thus far.

So let me introduce you to the storyteller.

I was born Jacqueline Iris Daly, on 27 June 1952 at 0.45 a.m., the eldest child and only daughter of an Irish father and Yorkshire mother. It's only now, as I see those descriptions written upon the page, that I feel truly grateful for the choice I made. Yes, I do mean choice. In my current belief system, the child chooses their parents to learn their life lessons and hence access their life's purpose. As a child, I chose to think I had no choice in the matter, and that became a pattern of my life.

I believe that before coming here I accepted a mission to bring about world peace. The moment I was born, it was erased from my memory. For nearly fifty years I wandered in the wilderness before reconnecting with it. It's from this place that my story starts. I'd like to share with you, from a place of I, how the reawkening to my life mission unfolded and what strategies and tools I've used to make this dream a reality.

This book is an invitation for you to share part of my journey, and in your doing so I'm also grateful to be part of yours. I've been inspired by many things in my life. With people it has often been the telling of their stories, the sharing of their gifts and talents or travelling with them on part of their journey. At other times, nature shows me her beauty and I feel full of the wonders of this fantastic planet. It may be a satellite photograph from space, a visit to a beauty spot, the cleansing feeling of a rainy day, the excitement of thunder or a breathtaking sunset or sunrise. Watching with awe as a newborn lamb or calf unsteadily finds its feet for the first time. Sometimes it will be when I see a wood softly carpeted with bluebells or daffodils or smell the sweet scent of freesias or roses. On other occasions I'll respond to my fingers touching the trunk of an old yew, feeling at one with its cracked bark and craggy twists. Being at one with myself, with others and with my environment leaves me with a sense of peace, and it's from this place that I know I have plenty.

When I see the world as my mirror, I am truly inspired and grateful for the knowledge that I have the opportunities to heal every moment of the day. I also acknowledge that I have free will. This means I can choose to be awake or not and, if I am awake, then I can choose to heal or not. There is no judgement on whether I do, just an acknowledgement that it is my choice. For me, my time on this planet is all about choice and taking personal responsibility for my life and therefore my thoughts, words and deeds.

Each one of us will make our own journey and experience different situations and challenges in finding the person we were born to be. It is hoped that we will find our own inspirational voice during the course of this journey and creatively express it. When we choose to share it, it becomes our gift to the world.

During the following pages, I shall illustrate how I reconnected with my soul, Source, spirituality, wholeness, community, love, peace, acceptance, joy, compassion and play while honouring the pain, tears, depression, loneliness, emptiness and separation. I shall be sharing many of the 'tools' that I discovered along the way and referring to people and places without whose help and guidance I would not have discovered the woman I am today.

The story will start on New Year's Eve, 2001 and will take you up to the present day, 2008. It will refer back to my childhood, maidenhood, motherhood and grandmotherhood and bring you up to date with the acceptance of being the wise, older woman I am beginning to know and love. Yet the lessons are there for all to see and connect with, because this is not just a story of a woman's life, or even of a British woman's life. It's the story of a soul, a person's true self, which remembers that we are all one, where barriers between gender, race, sexuality, age, religion, abilities melt away and the joy of peace is a reality, no longer a dream.

Our heroine takes full responsibility for her memories of the life she has led, the choices she has made, and she fully accepts that anyone who has shared all or part of this journey may have different memories and realities to her. They are all truths, and maybe it's our reaction to them and the consequences of those actions that are the real truth. This story is told from a place of love, acceptance and gratitude for those fifty years of wandering through the wilderness and for the people and events that have touched this soul. So you are invited to join me on this journey in whatever way honours your path. Feel free to engage with the 'toolkit' exercises or not. Read from the beginning to end or dip in and out as you like, let it sit on the shelf till the time is right or even reject it. Whatever your choice, it feels good to have made the connection with you thus far.

So let the story begin...

Reawkening

AT THE AGE OF FORTY-NINE I BEGAN TO RECOGNISE MY true self, the person I was born to be. It was also at this time that I truly knew what loving myself and others unconditionally meant. I had been reawoken on all levels. And with that had come a sense of freedom. I now felt limitless, at one with all and with those with whom I connected. Well, most of the time. I'm human, after all. So on the not-so-good days I would remind myself that this was how I could feel, and on the bad days, which rarely seem to happen, I reminded myself to remind myself. It has never taken more than that to get me back to the place I call 'Being at One'. It is from this place that I can connect with the joy and peace. From here the world is my oyster; my springboard, my opportunity to love all beings and my environment unconditionally. It's an opportunity to fulfil my purpose: the mission I said 'yes' to all those years ago. I'd gone from being a warrior to becoming a peacemaker. I discovered there was only one place I could start from, and that was within me.

I'd like to take you back to New Year's Eve, 2001. It was one of the most glorious days. The sun was bright and hung low in a crystal blue sky. A few cotton-wool clouds were dotted about and a thin crust of snow lay on the ground. In hindsight, it was obvious that something quite magical was going to happen that day. The scene was set and yet I had no idea what was to unfold.

I had been invited to join a girlfriend on a week's holiday in Durnsley, Gloucestershire. She, along with some of her friends and family, had decided to go away over the New Year period, and as I was on my own she asked me to join them. We had all been scattered across the country for the Christmas celebrations and therefore travelled separately to our holiday home. I was the first to arrive and from the minute I got there, I felt at home. I remember running around the house, exploring and going 'wow'. As I peered around each door, I felt my eyes widening upon each new discovery. I had a childlike sense about me, with all the freeing qualities that brings. I had put aside my other roles – manager of IT contracts, mother of two adult sons, survivor of three past intimate personal relationships (one fairly recent), friend, confidante – and now I was able to see the adventure, the wonderment, the beauty, the 'wow factor'. I wanted to share that excitement and within moments I was on the phone to my friend. Despite my state of wonderment, I was trying not to give too much away, as I didn't want to spoil the surprise for them.

Apart from my friend, I had never met the rest of the group before, but when they arrived we just gelled. It was about three days into the holiday before I realised that we had not created any rules, divided tasks or allocated rooms. It all just happened and fell into place. I was the early bird and still am; maybe being born at 0.45 a.m. has something to do with it? I was always happy to unload the dishwasher and get breakfast on the go. As I usually went to bed earlier than the others, they seemed to do the clearing up and put the dishwasher on. It seemed to me that people found where they fitted in naturally and gravitated to what they did best. It was only later, when I was studying at Ruskin College, Oxford and we were discussing Marxism, that the phrase 'give what you can and take what you need' came up and I realised that was what we had done. We operated without ego. There was no comparing of who did what and how that equated. To my mind, there was a lot of giving and acceptance, and I'm not sure that it was all conscious.

The holiday continued, and it was on New Year's Eve that one of the group suggested we go for a walk. He had identified a circular walk that would take us most of the daylight hours but would get us back in ample time to prepare for our evening's celebrations. We were happy to go along, so, dressing warmly, we packed our provisions. Armed with a map and compass, my new-found friend led the way. I remember how comfortable I felt with his masculine energy, and I was happy to follow and wondered why I noticed that feeling.

Now, I can see that he was comfortable with who he was and therefore I was, too. Also, I was beginning to notice the changes in me. His male power was different from those I'd been previously attracting. I was beginning to see the power that comes from within the gentleness, starting to see the soul of another person rather than their gender. I was seeing his gifts and talents first, and they were just what was needed at that time. There was another shift: I was slowing down and becoming a witness to what was happening, and from this place I was responding. Responding was something new. Previously I would have been reacting from a different space, a different me. It would have been a space from where an old, no-longer-needed programme was running.

The day was mostly like any other with a group of friends walking across the countryside. It was a very happy, joyful day and I remember a lot of laughter and kindness. We stopped around three in the afternoon and took out our flasks for a cup of something warm. From our high vantage point, we were able to observe the beauty of the scene around us. We were excitedly chatting about the plans we had made for the evening's celebrations. It had been decided previously that we would have a dinner party game – a Whodunnit. Weeks earlier, we had received information advising us of the theme and our character. We had also been asked to bring along some clothes to fit our role. After discussing what we had brought and who we were going to be, trying very hard not to give too much away, I was again reminded of that childlike, carefree feeling. It was beginning to feel like one of the best New Years I had ever had. Forget the boozy parties, I was thinking. This felt so fresh and new.

As the sun started to set, an icy breeze began to pinch our faces. It was decided that we had better set off again if we were to get home before it got dark. Reminiscent of a crocodile of children, we started to march down the hill in order to cross the edge of the golf course, on our way back to the cottage. The gaps between us had grown larger and I was bringing up the rear when something seemed to pull me and I turned to look to my right. I wanted to call out to the others, but I couldn't move. My world was frozen and had become silent. The skyline was breathtaking. It was amazing! The sun was bigger than I had ever witnessed. All I could see were multitude shades of reds and oranges. It was as if I were seeing colour for the first time. In a way, I knew I was.

Where the sun ended, the sky began with its streaks of cold blue, light orange and wispy white. I was alone in this universe and yet I felt so loved.

It was then that I heard the word 'community' as clearly as you see the word written on this page. Its clarity took me from my stillness and I looked around, yet there was no one there. I was being called now by the others, but at that moment I felt I had been called by God, a word that wasn't really part of my vocabulary. All I could see was the beauty and that I was part of it.

As I write now I am smiling, remembering those same feelings. Feeling the oneness with life, with myself, with God, and the joy of being so alive and so still at the same time. For the first time in my life, I had connected to the beauty and peace within, and it was from this place that the next part of my journey would start.

As the sun gently slipped down, I was brought back by the call of my friends who were huddled together, waiting for me at the bottom of the hill. We had been walking all day, but I now felt re-energised as I skipped downward to catch up with them. At the time, my experience wasn't something I felt I could explain to my friends. I was also aware that part of me wanted to hold onto it. I wasn't ready to share it or release it. Over the next few days, thoughts whirled around inside me.

'Community'. Why that word? Why had it been said to me? What did it mean? Why now? What was I supposed to do with it? It was a word that would repeatedly come back to me over the next few years. Each time, it took me back to that moment, to the beginning, to the time of my reawkening.

At the end of the week, when it was time for us to go our separate ways, I had a sense of what 'community' was and how wonderful it felt. I hadn't realised how alone I'd been. Not so much in the physical sense, but more in the sense of belonging. Many times in my life I had felt a lack of belonging. When I was young, I often thought there had been a mix-up at the hospital and that I'd been given to the wrong family. Everybody around me seemed different. This feeling became a pattern in my life for many years.

A month later, back in the office, that word came back to me again. My friend, with whom I had gone on the holiday, was working with me at the time, and on opening the post one morning she brought an advertising flyer to my attention.

'I think this is just up your street,' she said.

It was an opportunity to study 'Women's Studies' at Ruskin College in Oxford. Although it spoke to me, it was a particularly busy time at work, so I didn't do anything about it until a second copy of the flyer came to me via another channel of the organisation. By now I was getting the message. I was supposed to go there.

But how could that be? It would mean giving up my job. And what about all the financial implications that would have?

Having recently split up from my partner of ten years, I was still recovering from the sense of loss and grieving for the end of that relationship. Here I was now, contemplating giving up my job, my home, my income. What was I thinking of?

Gradually, it dawned on me that maybe it was the answer to my silent prayers. As a sixteen-year-old, I had wanted to go to university. This would have necessitated my staying on at school to do some A levels. Maths was the only subject I felt confident in (I didn't need to write words with maths; well, not many, anyway). I had put my heart and soul into all my other subjects and never could understand why it wasn't appreciated or why my grades were so low. It was always a surprise to me. Yet everything back then seemed to be stacked against me. I was receiving messages such as:

'Education is wasted on girls. They get married and have children. Why don't you become a secretary? You haven't exactly shown that you are university material.'

But I had so wanted to go. I can't verbalise what was driving me, but something was. Alas, it wasn't to be. It certainly wasn't for the want of trying, though. I must have driven my parents and teachers mad with the constant begging. I did manage to get parental permission to stay on for an extra year at school – as long as I took a secretarial course. This would mean that I would split my education between part-time school and part-time college. I jumped at the chance of more education, especially going to a mixed college after being at an all-girls school. I am grateful to my maths teacher, who, when I told her I wanted to get an 'A' level in maths in one year, did try her best to see if it could happen within the school. Unfortunately, the answer again was 'no'. She gave me one bit of advice that I will never forget. Although it was in relation to sitting a maths exam, I have used it on many occasions since.

She said, 'Always go with your first answer.' It has served me well over the years in many ways, especially now, when listening to my inner guidance. I see it as encouragement to trust myself.

I did well on the course; I even came out with a Grade 1 in Commerce and passed all my secretarial subjects, too. I was pleased to know I was good at something. I left school and college on the Friday and started my job as a secretary on the Monday. I was only there a few weeks before I realised that it was the job on the other side of the desk that I would like to have. I didn't have the qualifications, though. The guy I worked for at the time was receptive to my desire to learn more about his job and was willing to share his skills. I'm pleased to say that 'not having qualifications' has never stopped me going for a job since. I would look at the skills and qualities required, and if I wanted the job and felt that I could do it, then I'd ignore the fact that I didn't have the paper qualifications and apply. I do regard qualifications as a valid way of representing capabilities, learning and understanding. What I would add, though, is that it is just one way. Thankfully, the people who have employed me over the years must have thought so, too.

A month after seeing those flyers, I was on my way to Oxford for a Ruskin College Open Day. It wouldn't do any harm to look, I thought. Look! I was hooked from the moment I walked in the door, despite the first person I met.

What had attracted me there? he asked.

'Women Studies,' I said, smiling.

'Oh, that will probably not run. It didn't last year.' His shaking head spoke back at me.

'Don't put that message out.'

The response seemed to spill from my mouth involuntarily. I had imagined other women like me, from all around the country, wanting to give up everything to come and do Women's Studies.

There he was, putting out this negative energy and encouraging me into other subjects. It was a wonder I ever got accepted as a student.

He did look a bit taken aback at my response. I'm grateful I didn't let him put me off, because as I looked at the other subjects I knew that I was meant to be there. Women's Studies had been the hook, the bait, but now I was like a kid in a sweet shop. I was particularly drawn to Creative Writing but couldn't understand why. It was as if it came out of nowhere. I heaved a sigh of relief when I saw that taking the course required submitting an example of my work. I didn't have any, so I could rule that one out. There was so much on offer that I was spoilt for choice. I wanted to do it all, not just the studying but also living with a group of people who wanted to learn. The word 'community' came into my head again.

Seven months later, when I stepped into that college, I would experience that feeling of community for myself. My spiritual path was widening and I was beginning to get to know the real me. I felt I was making choices from a place of 'I' – from the very centre of my being. I was also being drawn, and I was choosing to go with the flow. I was on an adventure. I was creating a relationship with freedom.

I've noticed how what I refer to as the 'hook' or the 'bait' has played out many times in my life. I may have attended a course for one reason, only to find I had been led onto something else that maybe I wouldn't have chosen to do. It makes me feel that 'God' knows me very well, too well sometimes. It also helps me feel that spirituality doesn't have to be serious. There is room to have some fun around it, and it encourages me to take it lightly. It's not that I don't respect it; I do. For me it is the same as having food to feed my body: so spirituality feeds my soul. I like to think I take a 'healthy eating plan' attitude to it. It is just a thing I do daily, like breathing. I don't make a big song and dance about breathing every day. I accept it as an every-moment occurrence. I like to think the same way about spirituality – it's just like breathing and eating. Having a healthy approach to it is fine, but if I can't enjoy it then what can its purpose be for me?

Appropriately, it was nine months from that New Year's Eve

that I started my new-found life. The seed had been sown. The moment of conception was so blissful. Gestation had taken place. My birth into the world of Community had started.

A holistic holiday to Skyros kicked it off before I moved on to my new community life at Ruskin College. This was followed by a further year studying, living and working in the Findhorn Community in Scotland. Subsequently, I have experienced smaller family communities living on the island of Krk, Croatia; Reading, Berkshire; Ashbury, Oxfordshire, and then in South Wales.

It is true that I am being led. I have chosen to surrender and become a willing disciple of love, peace and joy. I started this journey having no idea where it was going. I would soon realise that at last I was going to university. I had enrolled into the University of Life. The course syllabus was unfolding with each new step I took.

I can now use the word 'God' and know what its essence means to me. I remember the qualities of the day that allowed me to hear the voice within for the first time. I was deep in the presence of beauty. It was from that place of stillness, of oneness that I became a willing heart for Source to work through. It would, however, be another two years before that understanding would come to me. One thing I did know at the time was that I was filled with love and a knowledge that had previously been hidden from my consciousness. That beautiful day was my time of awakening.

I was remembering.

***** Exercises *****

What have been the magical moments in your life? Why not list a few of them and reconnect with how you were feeling at that time? What was alive for you? Do you have enough of these moments in your life? How long does their magic last? What happens when it goes? Is it always there?

Have you had any moments in your life when you felt you were seeing or hearing something for the very first time? What were they? List the feelings those memories rekindle. Did they change your thinking or actions?

Are you willing to attract magical moments into your life now? The invitation is for you to be open for this to happen to you now. Allow yourself to be willing to experience situations anew. Keeping a journal or making notes helps. Write down daily for a period of time all you can remember feeling and experiencing. It may be when you go for a walk, when you see a film or when you are with your child or partner. Don't discount anything. Allow the feelings and memories to flow through.

What does the word 'spirituality' mean to you? Does your belief system allow for a sense of Source, God, Buddha, Mother Earth, Universe, Love or Oneness? Do you align with one or all of those words or do you have another one that is more appropriate for your beliefs? What do you feel about something connecting us all, something that is limitless, of which there is a spark inside all of us? How does spirituality play out in your life? Do you have a spiritual practice (something you do daily that connects you to the centre of your oneness, such as Tai Chi, meditation, yoga, prayer, etc.)?

Have you experienced 'hook/bait' scenarios? What unexpected opportunities/gifts have come your way because of them? Why do you think they happen? Consider whether there would have been any fear or resistance to the new learning or opportunity had the bait not been there. Look out for it in the future.

Have you ever let lack of qualifications stop you going for a job/course you wanted? Was that a realistic response? Did you think you could do it? If not, what were the qualities of the job/course that attracted you? Could those qualities that you recognise within you be fulfilled by another means? Would you be willing to attract an opportunity for you to express them? How would you do that both physically and spiritually?

List any unfulfilled childhood dreams. Feel into each one of them. Do any of them still have some energy for you? Could there be an insight to your life's purpose? Can you take one step today towards one of those dreams becoming a reality? What would it feel like to take that step? While honouring the first feeling that comes up, allow time for other feelings to surface. Honour all of the feelings that come up for you.

A Soul's Journey

As a child attending a Roman Catholic school, I had heard the word 'soul' many times. However, I think the first time I was ever touched by its meaning was on my second visit to the Findhorn Community, in Forres, Scotland. As part of the programme I was going to take part in my first ever Transformation Game™ and, true to my nature, I was taking it all very seriously. In brief, the game, as the name suggests, is about personal, group or planetary transformation. Taking an intention into the game, in the form of a sentence, allows the transformation to play out. I spent some time the evening before the game contemplating the statement, my intention, which I wanted to take into the game. The following morning, I awoke around 5 a.m. with a serious question in mind. I decided to ask for some help and guidance. I was working with Diana Cooper's Angel cards at the time, and I did not appreciate what I considered to be a flippant response. I was so angry that I threw the card across my bedroom.

After breakfast, I had some free time before the game started, so I went to sit in the sun room. It was while I was there, processing what had happened and feeling the warmth of the sun on my body, that I had this strange realisation. It seems difficult now for me to describe in words what I felt when I discovered I was a soul. In some ways, there are no words. Well, not in the vocabulary that I'm now using to communicate with you. Because it seems as if it's a place where words are no longer necessary. It was as if I were being touched for the very first time. Everything disappeared; I was fragmented and went beyond the limits of my human body. I was still me but was no longer constrained within my humanness with its shape, colour, gender, age, capabilities or emotions. I had become limitless in every sense. I was filled with, and was, love. It was as if all of me were the most beautiful smile you had ever seen. I was smiling from the inside out. I also perceived the sense of being 'at home', no longer separated. For me, the two human experiences that draw the nearest parallels to it are when I am being touched by a lover, or when I visualise the faces and recall memories of my children. I suppose that isn't so surprising, as with both of those examples there is a time when you share each other's bodies and seem to be as one.

It was also the first occasion on which I truly acknowledged the Christ energy. As a child I would often walk around a church, particularly at Easter time, and stand in front of each of the 'stations of the cross', looking up, as if the person there were someone I knew. Yet I rejected its truthfulness. At my core, I never rejected its essence, but I did choose to see the religious organisations and people who were part of them as poor representatives of what I felt I knew. I wasn't able to see the beauty through their harshness. At times over the years I would be drawn back, but nothing touched me as it had done now. I had been able to experience the beauty of other philosophies, beliefs and faiths, but it felt as if the jury were still out on the Christ energy. I was in denial. I'm noticing now how difficult it is for me to write the word 'Christianity' without feelings surfacing, such as pain and fear. As I write, tears are gently releasing themselves, caused by my association with the words 'persecution' and 'crucifixion' which seem to surface along with the word 'Christianity'. Interestingly, I'm writing this chapter in Holy Week, the days leading up to the crucifixion and the subsequent resurrection.

So what was I supposed to do with this new-found awareness, and why here and now? I've noticed over the last six years or so that the biggest shifts in my spiritual awareness have come at times when I have felt safe and joyful. I spent a lot of my life feeling very frightened and isolated, probably not very apparent from other people's perception because, being a Cancerian, I usually had my hard shell on view. Apart from the feelings of love and oneness I was experiencing in that sun room at Findhorn, I was also filled with a sense of peace, the serenity of which I had never known before. It felt so good after all the years of battling to be able to let go, to rest and feel held as if in strong loving arms. Nothing was going to touch me now except this love. I could just be and enjoy its gentle magnificence.

I don't know how long I stayed in that state, but when my awareness returned to the sun room I took up my pen and wrote the following poem line by line without stopping.

> I asked a serious question and he answered me with 'fun'
> It was the biggest one I'd ever asked and his answer felt like a shun
> I cried the tears of sadness because I'd asked for help before
> But he never came it seemed to me and it hurt me to the core
> But to play the 'hard and done by girl' no longer works for me I know
> Again I look at what it says and trust it's from a friend not foe
> So I accept the word and take to it for I cannot pick and choose
> To believe in him as I do I know I cannot lose
> It's been difficult for me at times to accept without understanding
> But the truth I feel will come to me in the journey not in the landing
> So I step into the golden light no longer feeling anger or blame
> I shrank before him from adult to child and into my heart he came
> All the years just melted away behind me. I was left with a feeling of faith
> Faith that I will understand, faith that I will grow
> But until the time is right for me I have faith to go with the flow
> It has brought me to a beautiful place where all in my heart seems right
> I choose to give myself complete; no longer afraid, I don't fight.
> So in celebration of today I dedicate myself to Fun

And in the words of the Carpenters, 'I've only just
begun'
So I'll remember to treat things lightly, be humorous,
joyous and at one
Be myself with the people around me and honour
this goddess of fun.

It was such a loving message – nothing was being asked of me except to have fun, to lighten up. It seemed that in that space I was able to let go of the burdens of responsibility which, it appeared to me, I had carried from within my mother's womb. I was now able to feel the lightness of life, the joyfulness, its peace and its love. I became the child I had never been and loved tapping into the playfulness. I was filled with gratitude that I no longer had to be the warrior. I discovered the true essence of choice and it was so peaceful. It was as if I no longer had to prove myself – I was myself, and I was beginning to love the 'me' who was emerging. I had surrendered. It was like a rebirth, and I was truly being touched for the very first time in the most loving of ways. I was wanted.

Wouldn't that be a wonderful way for a child to enter the world? To instantly bond with the love, peace, acceptance it had just left and to knowingly surrender to its beauty. I would love to think that there will come a time when this is the way we choose to celebrate the birth of our children. The experience of giving birth to my firstborn was far removed from that, but I was able to learn from its lessons for the birth of my second child.

The day my second son was born was one of the happiest of my life. I felt totally in control. It all started early in the morning, when I chose to keep my elder son home from his nursery group. This was going to be the last day he and I would be alone together in the way we had been for the past three years. From today onwards there would be two children to love, and I wanted to cherish those last hours with my firstborn. We played a lot of cowboys-and-Indians games; thankfully, these allowed for a lot of whooping noises, which acted as a great disguise when my labour pains kicked in. I was so grateful that my second son decided to hang on until the evening so that I was only separated from my elder son overnight. When we got back from the hospital the next morning, I remember my firstborn, on returning from his overnight stay with his nanny and granddad, jumping up onto my bed with the most huge smile and saying, 'Oh, Mummy – he's come.' It was said with so much love that I thought his little heart might burst out of his body.

He cradled his baby brother in his arms. It's good to be able to have those happy memories, because at the time my marriage was on the rocks and it was just three months later that their father and I separated. Over the years, the pain of not being able to remain a family together for them and myself has sometimes seemed unbearable and, knowing what I know now, a part of me wished I had healed before bringing them into the world. Another part of me accepts that I did the best I could with the skills I had at the time. No doubt my sons chose me and their father in order to be able to learn their lessons as I am learning mine.

So here I was, in the sun room at Findhorn, being touched in such a loving way that any guilt or judgements I had previously had were washed away. I was being given a new slate, it seemed. The choice was mine, and I decided to grab it with both hands. After all, this part of my journey commenced at the age of forty-nine, when I decided I could potentially have more of my life to live than I had already lived. That awareness certainly was a self-motivator for exploring how I might want that to unfold. It was an opportunity to find out who I really was and how I would like to express that over the rest of my life. With the advent of my new limitless self, my previous boundaries had disappeared; I no longer felt constrained by them, and I began to remember the visualisation I had when I saw myself speaking to a huge room full of people, my hand placed on the book I'd written. Who was to say I couldn't write that book and others too, or that I couldn't be the change I wanted to see in the world? Not me, for sure, and not the new energy I had connected with at that time. This new-found energy felt as if it were within and without me. I didn't hear any 'no's'; just an inner voice that said 'go for it, Jacqueline, go for it.'

I want to be part of a peaceful, loving world where everyone is appreciated for the gifts and talents they offer and everyone feels free to reach out for the help and support they need and have it generously and unconditionally responded to. It's a world that knows no fear and where abundance is the accepted norm.

It wasn't long before my blissful feeling started to disappear and my humanness kicked in again, and I began to feel separated, alone and fearful. When I tried to reconnect, I could, but it was how to carry it with me 24/7 that was the mystery. I think the main reason for this was that, although I was happy with this new-found knowledge, my humanness in the guise of my ego started to taunt me. 'OK,' it would say, 'so who are you going to tell this to? Remember what you feel about the "God Squad" and all those "evangelical" types. You don't want to be one of those, do you?' So this new knowledge became like a secret lover, and I was like a young girl again with a boyfriend whom my parents, family and friends wouldn't understand and accept. Not only that, but I also felt I would be ridiculed, maybe ostracised. So the experience was hidden from view, even from me. It was as if it had been placed in a tabernacle, and there it remained until my next visit to Findhorn a couple of months later.

On this occasion, my stay was to last for a month. Like most stays at Findhorn, I meditated on what my purpose would be for that period and discussed and formulated it with my focaliser. When I was silent and connected with my purpose, I was initially shocked at what came in, so much so that I couldn't even repeat all of the words. It felt so alien to my belief system at that time that I wondered where the words had come from. After spending two hours dialoguing and processing, eventually I was able to say that I felt my purpose for that programme was 'I am a channel for Jesus Christ, and through me passes his love.' Firstly, the word 'channel' made me feel awkward. I heard a voice inside me say, 'Don't you think you're getting a bit above your station? – and, by the way, all your friends and family will think you really have lost it.'

Then I spent an hour unable to utter the words 'Jesus Christ'. All I kept saying to my focaliser was, 'I don't do that stuff. You know. Religious stuff.'

Bless her, she hung on in there with me, asking questions,

accepting my answers, and I thought I was there when I was able to come up with the idea of calling him JC. My response, when asked why that worked for me, was that it sounded more funky and acceptable. She wasn't having it, though, because she asked me whether the message came through as JC or Jesus Christ. Well, she had me there – she was good.

I was remembering my previous visit and what had happened for me then, and recalling the beauty of it. It was at that time that a childhood school memory came to me and I was reminded of one of the things that Jesus said to his disciple Peter: 'Assuredly I say to you that today, even this night, before the rooster crows twice, you will deny me three times' (Mark 14:30). I felt as if I were Peter; even though I knew in my heart of hearts that my purpose was a truth, I was denying it to protect myself, so as not to be ridiculed or persecuted. I was denying the beauty I had connected with. Not only that, but I was also denying myself. I was that beauty too. So eventually, after working through the issues and prejudices, I was finally able to state my purpose and know that I meant it from the heart. I was grateful for the work my focaliser had put in with me. I was also grateful that I had used my free will to examine and understand my fears and challenges. A part of me was thinking that I was not worthy, another part felt that anyone who said those words was being egotistical, and the most joyous part of me felt 'wow, what a way to spend your life, being a channel for unconditional love'. If I could be like anybody, then why wouldn't I want to be someone like Jesus? Someone who spent their time travelling around, speaking with and listening to people: teaching, learning from, empowering and supporting people to heal? What an inspirational person he was – what a role model. I was at peace again and full of love. It was as if the tabernacle door had been once again opened.

No sooner was I in a state of acceptance than the fear returned as before. If I was linked with the Christ energy, wouldn't that mean I was separate again from my fellow beings that followed other belief systems? The Christians I had come across said mainly that their way was the right way and if you followed Christ then there was no other. I was remembering parts of the Roman Catholic Catechism, not verbatim, but the gist of what I felt I was indoctrinated with as a seven-year-old: 'I will not hold any other graven images or idols before Thee.' I was remembering that when I was a Brownie of around eight years of age that I was not allowed with the other children into the church on parade days; it would be wrong for me to go into the Church of England church, as I was a Catholic. I had to wait outside while my fellow Brownies went in. I didn't want anyone to have to feel like that little girl.

It was then I recalled my first ever visit to Findhorn during Experience Week. I had managed to meditate, something I had never done before, heard a weed scream when being pulled from the ground and was about to look for the guys in white coats coming to take me away when I was hit with a back problem and spent the rest of the week mostly lying flat out. On one of my early morning visits to the kitchen to refill my hot water bottle, I was drawn to a card on the noticeboard from a member of the Foundation called Franco Santoro. I didn't know him, nor had I heard of him, but I just knew he would be able to help me. Unknowingly, I was beginning to work with my intuition. I left him a note and the next day I was having my first session with him. Among many things, he works with Astroshamanism, and during a conversation with him I decided to go on a shamanic journey. It was during this journey that I got glimpses of all religions and belief systems, together in one place, side by side. It felt good to see it that way. That experience, once integrated, allowed me to release any separation from those who were Buddhists, Muslims, Jews, Pagans, Atheists, etc. What this experience was now allowing me to do was adding the Christ energy to the list, not discarding the rest.

I found, during my stay at Findhorn and many times since, that nothing can separate me from anyone else, my soul or Source except me. I often attended events that were organised along Buddhist lines and meditated only to find I had Buddha and Jesus coming in at the same time. Having them 'hang out together' would please me. The same would happen with Pagan events, when I was able to appreciate Mother Earth and nature. I have attended many places of worship and ritual, be they Spiritualist, Mormon, Salvation Army or traditionally Christian. I have celebrated Beltane and honoured my ancestors, calling them in from all the directions of the compass, from upper, middle and lower worlds, and I have worked with archangels, healing spirits and guides and ascendant Reiki masters. It appears to me that I am able to find that place where another's beliefs and mine meet, rather than separate us. At this time of writing, my philosophy is that all holistic belief systems and religions journey to the same place, and I call that Source. It is a place of love where I can be at one with myself and with those around me. It has both an inner and outer function and connects us all to whatever we choose to call it.

As I started to get used to connecting with my soul and Source, I noticed that it wasn't being locked in the tabernacle so often. We were 'hanging out' together and forming a relationship. Part of my question, asked earlier on in this chapter, was 'Why here?' Well, Findhorn is the place to find out answers, even to questions you haven't thought of asking. Its function is definitely not to promote the Christ energy or any one belief system. It's bigger than that. It holds a space in which to find one's own truth, whatever that truth may be. All are welcome, and the only rule I found was about respect – respecting oneself and those around you. It is hugely diverse, yet there is a silken thread that runs through and connects all. It was my home and family for a year and I'm happy to return to check in with folks when I'm in the area. Looking back on my life, I can see that different threads were leading me to Findhorn, so in some ways it was predestined and I was definitely happy to arrive there.

Following on from my year at Ruskin, Findhorn felt like the second year of my 'make up your own' degree. I was like any other form of energy; I needed to be refuelled, and Findhorn was my soul's 'petrol station'. Boy, was I thirsty when I got there. As with my time at Ruskin, I was again a kid in a sweetshop with all the goodies in front of me. I had time to explore and taste to see what would nourish me. I was beginning to know why, when I had previously met William Bloom and Findhorn came up in our conversation, he couldn't describe it to me, other than to say, 'It is such a personal experience that it could never be the same for any two people.'

And he was so right.

It was a safe environment in which to 'hang out' with my soul. Nobody batted an eyelid at the words I might use or when I shared what I was experiencing. I certainly wasn't alone or isolated, and the 'real me' started to bloom and blossom in this haven. There was room for me to be as big as I wanted to be. I no longer had to shrink to fit the straitjacket I had been wearing. I even got brave enough to test my thoughts out on a few of my friends who were not part of the Community and received understanding and acceptance. Surprisingly enough, these friends were now free to express their own spiritual/holistic approach to life to me. A couple of friends even came up for a visit.

One member of my family, however, found the new me and the way I was living my life a bit hard to cope with. I love him all the more for being so truthful with me and, more importantly, for being true to himself. When he told me how he felt, I remember thinking that it was the best conversation I'd ever had with him. I can't deny there was pain, too, and the tears just rolled down my face, but all I felt was love for him and I had no doubt that behind what he was saying was love for me too.

It was during a three-month event called the Findhorn Foundation Programme that my heart chakra was opened even wider. I no longer felt that my soul had been put away into its tabernacle. I was the tabernacle and its door was always open.

As part of the programme, we were to spend a week on the beautiful island of Erraid, just off the west coast of Scotland and near the island of Mull. Although I was mostly looking forward to the visit, I did notice in myself a certain amount of resistance to going to the island. I had also begun to learn that what I resisted most was often what would serve me best.

There were two main areas of resistance I identified. Firstly, it was the outside, compost toilets. This woman doesn't do camping, so the idea of going outside in the middle of night, in November, in wellington boots, with a torch, was not instantly grabbing me. My second resistance manifested itself in the form of my resentment towards a certain Caroline Myss. She was offering a workshop at Findhorn and, as was the norm for her work, she was attracting many attendees. This meant that the twenty beds that those of us on the programme were taking up needed to be released to accommodate them. When I see that written now, it makes perfect sense, but at the time I felt pushed out. We had been living in our rooms for nearly three months. We were then being asked to pack up all the belongings we had and store them while we were away so that the rooms could be re-used. Not only that, but we had to leave at 5 a.m. on our morning of departure, so in true Findhorn style we had to be up even earlier to ensure that our rooms were clean, beds made and energy cleared ready for the new people to arrive. Obviously there were several lessons to be learnt, and I am now grateful that they arose in that way so that I could process them.

Despite my resistance, I was off on the bus to Erraid, a bit blurry-eyed but a little bit more joyful at the suggestion that we could have a bucket in the shower room of the house we were staying in, which would save the middle-of-the-night jaunts to the outside loo.

It would be six months later before I was able to appreciate Caroline's work, when I had the opportunity to read her book, *Why People Don't Heal and How They Can*. Mainly, I think, because it reinforced my awareness of 'woundology' and how that operates. But that is another story.

The week at Erraid was absolutely wonderful on all levels. I even came to terms with the advantages of the compost loos. I don't know if the veil between the worlds is particularly thin there, but it seemed that there was an opportunity for me to go deeper on a spiritual level and it just presented itself to me without my even thinking about it. Considering we were there during the last week in November, the weather was glorious. I even managed a sunburnt nose.

It was midway through the week when the toilets appeared to come into their own. I was popping out for my early morning ablutions when I made my very first request to the Universe.

For most of my life I had chosen to recall only negative memories of my childhood, and this now struck me as being a bit selective. It dawned on me that I could allow positive memories to surface. I was hoping for a balance. I had the need for realignment in my consciousness.

Different words to describe this power I had started to work with randomly pop into my head. Sometimes it is Source, sometimes Universe and sometimes God. I seem to tap into the same place whatever name I use, and I believe that's because what is most important is intention. If my intention is from the heart and serves the highest good, then it is heard and answered. Maybe not always in the way I might expect it, but, hey, that's another lesson. What I've learnt to do with my requests is, once they have been voiced, to let them go and not to think or worry or control how they are going to be answered, just to know that they will.

Later that morning, as I was working in the pantry, giving it a top-to-bottom clean, I was aware of something happening between me and a friend of mine on the programme. Although we were working in different parts of the kitchen area and there wasn't a lot of conversation going on, I could feel this energy between us. I was aware that it was a very loving energy and I was interested in knowing why it had come up now. We had known each other for nearly three months and had been in a spiritual support group which met every week, but I'd never noticed the energy in this way before. Thankfully, he was busy in his work and didn't notice me looking and wondering what was going on.

When I returned to my house at lunchtime, I pondered on this experience, and I went into the silence and asked my soul what was happening. Within a few minutes of being in the stillness, I sensed a golden ball next to me and it felt as if it were my brother's soul. This appeared to answer my question concerning what type of love I was feeling for my friend. It was brotherly love. I don't know what had inspired me to ask the questions, but I was grateful that I had. Being fairly new in working from this place of Source, a place of love, I could have mistaken it for a boy-meets-girl situation. I was in one way relieved, as he was in a relationship with a friend of mine and it's one of my unwritten rules that you don't mess with a friend's partner. As it turned out, I was able to know it for what it really was and I'm happy to say we are still the best of friends. I was grateful to Source for steering me on that one. A year or so later, I had a past-life regression; the same friend was in that, and I could see again why there would be a love contract between us. It has since proved very useful to me, when working with this new-found 'love', to ask myself the question, 'What type of love is this? Is this feeling relevant to this life or another? Is there a Soul Contract I'm part of? What's my role this time around?'

Equally, it is worth noticing when something or someone triggers an adverse reaction in me. I allow the person or the incident to act as a mirror for me. I realise that it's always a gift and I have an opportunity to transform a part of me that I'm not embracing. Some call it our 'shadow' or 'dark side'. I have discovered that it isn't something to be afraid of but it will keep being triggered until I address it. I acknowledge these feelings as 'old ways' which no longer serve me. I look at the qualities of the attribute being triggered and not the action. It is then that I realise that I no longer wish to suppress that part of me. My desire now is to use the qualities in a different way. I remind myself that I am not whole until I embrace all of me.

The message that came to me that lunchtime, however, turned out to be twofold, because I realised that I was now able to connect to my youngest brother, who had passed over a few years before. He had come in response to my early morning question about allowing positive memories to arise. He was seven years younger than me. I hadn't always been the perfect 'big sister' when he was very young; I sometimes begrudged having to be responsible for him. Nevertheless, we were very close. Since his passing, I'd often seen him in my dreams, but there always seemed to be something between us, like a pane of glass, or we were separated across a large room or at the end of a telephone line. I believe now that was his way of connecting with me. But right there on the island of Erraid he was right next to me. Reminding me of the fun we had had together. He also told me that I was very special and that was why he had chosen me to be his big sister. Well, you can imagine that the tears were rolling down my face. He was a special person, too. He also experienced a lot of pain in his life, in childhood and later losing his first wife to cancer when she was only twenty-seven. Even though he did marry another beautiful woman, he never lost the bouts of depression that would set in at times. I had been able to talk him out of an attempted suicide once from 150 miles away down a telephone line, but when he did pass over there was no one around and, being a diabetic, he slipped into a coma. I don't know for sure if it was his intention to cease being in his body or not. What I did know was that he was no longer in his pained body and part of me was grateful for that. It was great to be so close to him again, and I was grateful to the Universe for the happy memories.

I do understand why when we find our soul and our connection with Source it comes with a health warning, 'be careful what you wish for', because my experience is that I usually get it. Another way I've heard that put is 'thoughts become things – choose the good ones'.

My experiences on Erraid were not over, it seemed; the following day we had a 'free day' and there was an opportunity to visit the island of Iona. From the first time I'd heard about it, especially in Mike Scott's (of the Waterboys) song, I'd always wanted to go there, but when the morning arrived I knew I just couldn't leave Erraid. Some force was holding me there. Not against my will, but something was encouraging me to hang around and be there when it was quieter. It was a beautiful day and I went for a lovely walk. I had this sense of being at one with the island and the sky and the sea. It was a wonderful feeling and I just let the day be what it was to be. I was remembering my own suicide attempt and the new beauty and oneness I had found. I had been given a new life on the day I attempted suicide, and I'd been given a new slate on an earlier visit to Findhorn. Now I was being given a new opportunity, one that I was instigating. It was on this day that I decided to offer myself up to Source. From that day forward I offered to give my life to service – however that might manifest. It was only later in the day that I realised that it had been exactly thirteen years ago to the day when I had attempted suicide.

On the night before we were to depart, we arranged a social event – a sharing. People were invited to play music, sing a song, share a poem, and afterwards we could dance or chill out.

It was a wonderful evening, and before I went a poem wrote itself for me. As the day was quite significant, I called the poem 'Surrender'.

Is thank you enough? I ponder when I look back over
the week.
Will my voice be heard and understood or will it need
a final tweak?
For a time now I've accepted him as part of my life
every day.
I've learnt to listen and I've chosen to do what I
thought I heard him say.
I thought our relationship was a wonder that truly
was complete,
But over the last few days he has knocked me off my
feet.
I've never felt such love before as I've done so
recently.
I never thought it was possible to let anyone that close
to me.
As I look back and appreciate his patience, his trust,
his belief
That I could learn to surrender and accept his love for
me.
So I feel now full of his passion, his love and the work
I choose to do
'Being me' is all he desires – a soul for his love to pass
through.
I knew there was a spark that twinkled inside of my
soul,
But now it's a flame burning brightly and some may
see its glow.
It may help to bring life to other sparks who are
searching for what they don't know,
And they too will become flames and others will then
see their glow.
Its aim is for compassion, for love, fun, joy and
delight,
For peace, gentleness and harmony, a chance to give
up the fight.
So it is with love and passion that I give my 'thank
you' a little tweak:

I'd like to add the word Beloved. A word I thought I
would never speak.
Thank you, Beloved.

Reconnecting with my soul and Source has literally changed my life. The frightened little girl inside me has been given time and the resources to heal and has blossomed into a beautiful young woman and then an equally beautiful older woman. I'm not arrogant enough to think that all the work is done. I'm definitely a work in progress, but I have grown so much and I appreciate the time I have given myself over the last few years in which to find me. I don't believe for one moment that my journey is 'the way', the journey that everyone has to take. If sharing my way inspires and encourages at least one other person to look and reconnect with their soul, their Source, and find the person they were born to be, then I'm grateful for the sharing. If the tools that have come my way are useful to another, then I'm grateful, because for sure they are not my tools. Nothing about my story is unique except for the fact that it is my story. The tools, the awareness, the experiences are all messages sent from Source to all of us. All we need to do is tune into the right frequency or hitch up with someone else who has, until we find the right channel for ourselves. Every message I get from Source I believe is a message for all. That helps me know how special we all are. When I heard that being me was what served him best, it enabled me to look at everyone else knowing that he had said that to them, too.

I'm filled with gratitude to my soul and Source for waiting so patiently for me to reconnect. I am constantly reminding myself of that when I'm rushing along my new-found pathway, eagerly wanting to work from the place of Source within and to see and respond to the Source in another. I rarely feel the pain of loss or separation or the need to look externally for gratification or praise.

'I AM' is my new mantra.

At the beginning of this chapter and in other parts of this book, I have shared with you the impressions I received as a child with regards to my interpretations of my religious upbringing in the Catholic Church. I'm blessed to be able to share with you now a more recent experience which helped me to balance those earlier understandings. When we ask God, the angels or ascended masters for insights and experiences we are always answered even when we can't always remember the asking.

During September 2007, I visited Pluscarden Abbey in Morayshire. I had no intention of going there and if I had known at the time of its recommendation that it was of the Roman Catholic faith I wonder if my old programmes would have rejected the idea out of hand. I had offered to drive a friend to the Findhorn Community in Scotland where she was to attend a two-week course. Having lived there previously I felt sure I could find someone to stay with during the visit. Can you believe it? Nothing was coming up. Four days before we were to set off from South Wales a friend from Findhorn suggested Pluscarden and I got online straight away. I had always meant to go there when I lived in Findhorn but had never made it, so the suggestion intrigued me. I learnt that the monks were mostly silent, only using words when it was necessary, so my communication with them was via email. I had suggested to my friend that we break our journey to Findhorn at Dunfermline as I had a friend from my Findhorn days there and he would be happy for us to stop over to break our journey. It was only when we arrived at his home, the evening before we were to arrive in Findhorn, that I received an email from Pluscarden inviting me to come to stay.

Pluscarden is home to a community of Benedictine monks. As I had no idea why I was to be staying there I opened my heart to the experience. I decided to go to the six daily gatherings they held in the abbey. On the second morning at 4.45 a.m. I attended what they call Vigils and Lauds. I had enjoyed all the gatherings the day before and was particularly drawn to this session. The voices of the monks really touched my heart and I heard myself ask a question: 'How can men's voices sound as beautiful as this?' And as clear as the words on this page an instant answer came back, 'When you know my love and offer it to me. That's what it sounds like.' I knew without a doubt that God had spoken to me again and he had chosen to do this inside the walls of a Roman Catholic abbey. I felt instant release. I felt that there was now a balance, for me, with regards to my experiences and the Roman

Catholic Church. I knew I would no longer need to tell the tales of horror of my childhood interactions or attract stories that would reinforce those earlier experiences. I had now experienced both ends of the spectrum and I felt aligned. I even enjoyed taking part in the Mass the following day even though I didn't take the sacrament. I knew that the love of the Divine that I knew was within those walls too.

***** Exercises *****

What does the word 'soul' mean to you? Don't feel you need to limit yourself to a written response. Explore other ways you can express it; be as creative as you want to be; maybe by drawing, painting, dancing, making sounds. If you are not sure about your relationship with the word, why not just ask the question and see what comes back?

Do you feel constricted by boundaries that no longer serve you? What would the picture look like if you were to redraw these boundaries? What shape and form does your boundary take? What would be inside and what would be out? Who would be inside and who would be out? How does it feel to have people outside? What changes would need to happen so that there wasn't a sense of separation? Remember you can't change anyone else; you can only transform yourself.

If you were to be a channel, whom or what would you channel? Feel into the qualities, the attributes, and try not to judge or censor what comes to you; allow it to flow and speak to you. Be on the lookout for further connections and notice the times and places when the connections work best for you. Remember we are all different and work in different ways and at different speeds. If nothing comes, leave it for a while. Trust that you will know when to ask again.

Have you ever tried automatic writing? Why not play with it when you have time? Ensure a quiet space and just let your pen lead you. You can start with a question or statement and see what flows. You may even find that you have a conversation with your Source. (Alternatively, you can also try this with a musical instrument, or paints, or your voice; remember you are limitless.)

When you are attracted to someone and feel a huge essence of love, why not ask yourself what type of love this is? You may find you have had a connection in a previous life, or the person is a trigger for a healing experience. The answer doesn't necessarily preclude you from having a relationship, but it might help you not to have an unhealthy one. It's worth remembering that this can work the other way, too.

Notice what triggers you adversely in another. Can you identify incidents in your life where that has played out? If you are willing, turn the incident around and see how you may act out in that way, too. Identify the qualities that have been triggered and see how you may wish to use them differently.

What experiences have you had with connecting with friends and loved ones who have passed over? Have they come to you in your dreams? Do you sometimes sense a smell that triggers a memory? Do you feel a blowing on your cheek or a tingle at the back of your neck? If it is something you are happy with, acknowledge them. They are not there to frighten you. They are there to reassure you and sometimes to guide you. Pets can often come through in this way, too.

Forgiveness

A Stepping Stone to Love and Acceptance

HAVING HEADED THIS CHAPTER 'FORGIVENESS', IT SEEMS ironic that the first thing I say is that forgiveness of oneself and others is all part of an illusion. For me, in an enlightened world it is totally unnecessary. However, for my journey it was an important stepping stone that led me to a state of acceptance. The freedom that forgiveness brought led me home to a place I call love. Over the years I've experienced various self-developmental events, counselling and therapy, and yet none has given me the lightness and the wings that came from the work I chose to do on forgiveness. I'd always felt that I was a person who could draw a line under anything and move on, so on the surface it could be assumed that I did not hold grudges and had been forgiving and held people in a place of love. However, unintentionally, I did a really good act of fooling myself and those around me. It really was a surface job, I realised: one in which I was an expert. I had become an expert in isolating my feelings, pushing them down to the very foundations of my being. There they had lain, frozen in the ions of time, in the glacier age of my existence until I reconnected with my spirituality.

Very slowly, they were triggered one by one and rose to the surface. Similar to an iceberg, I had only dealt with the ten per cent I could see. The other ninety per cent below the surface was somewhere in my subconscious. Those feelings needed healing, too. Once triggered, they learned to demand my attention, yet sometimes they came without warning; bearing no signs indicating to what or whom they were connected. At first I felt helpless. I had no idea what part they had played in my life. Were they friend or foe? Would they help or hinder me? I needed a way to engage with them. I would sit with the feeling and let my hands rest on the part of the body to which they were drawn.

It would be a few years later before I realised that my hands had gravitated towards my chakras for healing purposes. Learning Reiki and then becoming a Reiki Master/Teacher has been a great blessing.

I would then ask my body the questions I might want answers to, such as 'why is this feeling surfacing now? What has just happened that is connected with that memory? Please help me locate the memory this current feeling refers back to. Are there more memories that this feeling links to? Does it refer to memories in past lives? What is the fear? What is my current learning?' I learnt that if I worked in this way the triggers and insights I received served my life.

So forgiveness became the key that unlocked my jewelled case. The first time I really felt it was when I was at home, having breakfast before attending the second day of a Louise Hay course I had enrolled on. I was sitting there quietly with the sun shining through into the dining room, totally unaware of having any thoughts in my head. Suddenly, I felt as if there were something flowing out of my body and filling the room. It was similar to lava which had slowly and majestically left its volcanic womb, filling the space all around me. Looking back, I suppose I would liken the experience to a very strong visualisation. But not one I had consciously entered into. As it flowed, I heard myself ask my body its first question. Why I did it, I have no idea; it seemed to come quite naturally. I had asked what it was and I was answered with the word 'forgiveness'. I suppose it wasn't so strange that this should be the first feeling that arose as my partner and I were in the process of separating. What had been to me the most wonderful of relationships had turned sour and we had been unable to recapture its beauty. What was ebbing from me felt like all the hurts and negative feelings I'd been harbouring about my partner; the ones I had held onto because I thought he had hurt me. I had chosen to blame and judge both outwardly and to some extent inwardly instead of looking for the learning. The partnership had become a war zone and there were many casualties. We both had children and extended family; none of us had escaped without injury. It was also a relationship that, when I look back now, didn't have a solid foundation. For me, I guess the cracks that appeared were because it was a relationship based on dishonesty and, to some extent, guilt. When we had met, although I had not been in a relationship, my partner had been married. There were times when I felt as if I were part of the UN and was getting the fallout from all sides. I was trying to be neutral and then received blame for not taking what appeared to be one side against another. In trying to find a resolution for all those involved, I had lost the essence of me along the way.

I was feeling a huge sense of loss of family, love, unity, resolution, community, harmony, understanding and, of course, acceptance. A few years, later I was to be given a freeing message from a woman I was drawn to in Findhorn. It was being channelled through her for me, and the words were 'why fear loss?' I remember starting to give her an answer when she gently raised her hand. 'It is not given to you so that you can think of an answer. It is given to you as a statement of fact.' So many times during my life that message has come back into my awareness and it has always led me to peace. Often the loss of something has brought me something new; a new insight, a new opportunity a new home, a new friendship. Even the loss of a loved one to the other side has brought its miracles, too.

What surprised me most about the visualisation that morning was the colour of the lava that was flowing from me. As it was related to hurts and negative feelings, I would have expected the lava to be thick, black and slimy; instead, it was golden and light. It must have flowed for ten minutes or so; I lost track of time as I engaged with what was happening. I started to feel light and noticed that I had an inner and an outer smile. I was filled with joy. When I reflected, it felt as if I had unloaded a huge weight. What a burden it is to dislike or even hate someone, especially when it was someone I had learnt to love. I believe that when I accessed forgiveness it came to me as a gift. It wasn't something I had to work out for myself, to weigh up the pros and cons for; it was an inner wisdom, a memory of something I had always known. It was like discovering a concealed door to my heart and soul. I believe that was why it was instantly transformed into golden light. From that place, I would not have wanted to pollute the world with my negativity. When something is released from me now, I pray that it is recycled instantly into love. Something we can all benefit from.

My then-partner and I had separated in all ways except for the fact that we were still living in the same house. We had separate rooms, separate lives; we mostly avoided each other and were generally not communicating. During that time, I could barely look at him. To me he had become unrecognisable, even ugly and monster-like. Yet that morning, when he passed me to go to the kitchen, I was surprised to see the man I had learnt to love – the only man I had known romantic love with – looking back at me and for an instant I could have gone to him as I would have in the past. I yearned to look into his eyes, gently touch the back of his neck, twiddle his hair and kiss his lips. Forgiveness enabled me to return to love, to return to a state of grace.

Now, if I were to be faced with a similar situation, I would be able to utilise one of my new-found tools of 'mirroring'. It is as if Source has created everything else around us as a reflection for learning. I'm reminded of a saying I heard when on a holistic holiday in Skyros: 'All the people and all the events in our lives we draw to us. What we choose to do with them is up to us.' 'Learn' is my response to that now. So, if I were to look back at that situation, I would choose to look inward and see what was reflected back to me.

So I asked myself, what, then, were the parts of me which I felt were ugly and monster-like? Which were the parts of my lifestory I wished to review and forgive, especially in connection with how I had reacted to him and his family when our relationship had begun to die?

I started to see the scenarios clearly. All they needed were my invitation and willingness. What I needed was a place of safety to process this; a place where I knew I was loved and supported. I'd found that, on day one of the Louise Hay course. I had found the love of me from within me. I had connected with my beauty, which had been a long time sleeping, just waiting to be reawkened. From that place, I found the willingness to love myself. By means of the visualisation that morning, I had learnt to reconnect with the love for another, from the stepping stone of forgiveness. What really pleased me was how glad I felt to see my partner in his beauty again, and also to feel and see me in mine. They say beauty is in the eye of the beholder, and I think I needed to be reconnected with my beauty before I could truly see it in another.

I had grown up thinking I was ugly: a word someone used to describe me when I was about ten or eleven. I had chosen to believe that label until I was in my late forties. I had got into lots of arguments over the years for refusing to have my photograph taken. I would also avoid mirrors. Although I was now choosing to 'love myself and heal my life', as Louise puts it, a couple of years would pass before I would be able to finally eliminate the label 'ugly' as a description of myself. I wrote the word on a stone and threw it into the Mediterranean Sea. I haven't missed it at all. Eventually, I was able to look at myself in a mirror and tell myself how beautiful I was. To truly see the beauty, feel it and mean it when I said it. I've done quite a bit of mirror and mirroring work with myself and people who chose to work with me and can definitely recommend it as part of a healing process.

I remember using the mirror on another occasion, when I was facing the fear of singing in public. I was living at Findhorn and it came to me, as these things sometimes do, that I would reframe my relationship with fear. I had decided that, whatever fear arose, I would engage with it and see if I could work through it, if that was what felt appropriate. After all, I do have free will. Well, for years I'd only really sung when I was alone or if there were lots of other voices around me. Under no circumstances would you get me singing in public, on my own, out loud.

This particular fear really did want to play out, and it had decided that Findhorn was the venue. When I said to my focaliser that I was working with fear and that I wanted to dispel the one about singing in public, the Universe provided me with lots of opportunities to face it. The first was at an afternoon event to do with singing, which was programmed into the current course I was attending. Funny, that! I was feeling anxious before I got there, but I was definitely up for it.

'Right,' said the Universe, 'let's see how you handle an Aboriginal song.'

I'd been diagnosed as being borderline dyslexic at Ruskin and, as I hadn't seen the words before, it was difficult for me to make sense of them, let alone sing them. Having faced one fear, I was now being hit with another: my fear of not being able to read, understand and learn any words I've never seen before as quickly as others. While I was getting to grips with that, we were asked to put ourselves in our places in the singing group – alto, soprano, tenor or bass.

You've got to be joking, I thought. I've only just agreed to let a sound out, and now you're asking me which type of sound I am.

The Universe was not giving me the soft option. Fortunately, the group I was with knew about the challenges I was facing and helped to direct me. I couldn't have done it without them.

When the singing tutor said she was going to take the words away, I nearly flipped. I explained that I couldn't do it without them. It was hard enough for me to transpose the letters I saw in front of me into words at the moment, let alone remember them. Still she went ahead with it, and it was then that I felt my focaliser put her hand on my shoulder and I knew there was no way she was going to let go. I can't describe the pain I felt. It was as if every pain in my life time had risen at once, all the times I'd been humiliated, felt alone and unsupported, felt abused, been the victim. I was sure that the hand on my shoulder was allowing me to stand in my power and not run away this time. I'm sure she must have felt the pain I felt, gulped every inner sob and cried every silent tear. When the words were snatched away from the stand, I was taken back in time to when, aged four, my dummy was snatched from my mouth and thrown in the bin. Another very symbolic time when I'd hidden my loss, pain and anger. With my new-found skills and tools, I was grateful for the learning.

When the afternoon event had ended, friends came to support me and say how awful they thought the tutor had been. I was able to share with them the gifts I had received and how grateful I was for the experience. I had learnt to stand in my power, to offer up the best I had and release the fear of judgements and not being accepted. I sang the words I could remember, hummed the ones I couldn't and held my place of love for all concerned. The tears just rolled down my face and I felt that each was a pearl. They were tears that had been waiting for a long time to surface. I wasn't going to hold them back any more. I was remembering the answer I had received from a recent labyrinth enquiry. There is a belief that if you ask a question when you walk into a labyrinth, the answer will come as you journey outward.

'What is my purpose?' I asked as I entered the labyrinth.

'To bring joy and laughter from the release of tears,' was its response as I came out.

I wasn't at the joy and laughter stage just yet, but I knew it would come, when I was able to look back and see the lighter side of this experience. Seeing the lighter side of any experience has always enabled me to free myself from any stuck scenario. I often refer to my laughter chakra as my special chakra. It seems to free space for insights and love to come in.

It was a few days later when I met up with my focaliser again and said that, following on from that experience, I wanted to sing alone in front of an audience at one of the 'Cluny Unplugged' evenings that Findhorn hosts.

'I'll do it before Christmas,' I told her.

We were in August and she responded with, 'There's one this coming Saturday; why not do it then?'

Ugh! I loved that woman to bits, but surely she had to be joking. Thankfully, I knew her intention came from a place of love. I said I would think about it and went off for a walk. I took what she had proposed into a walking meditation. On the way back, I noticed that the path through the woods was covered in white feathers. I took this as a message to say I could do it. So the next thing was for me to decide on the song. It had to be 'Hero' as sung by Enrique Iglesias. He sings it as a love song to another person. I decided that I would sing it to myself by using a mirror. The words would reflect my new-found love for myself and the knowledge that I was my own hero. I'm sure that some people will cringe and think that this comes from a place of ego. I can assure you it does not. It was me holding my inner child and telling her all the things she had never heard before. I also believed that as I was singing it to myself, so I was singing it to my Source. It's the place we meet.

Nothing was stopping me now, so on another occasion I also sang 'What a Wonderful World' as a lead in to a group meditation in one of Findhorn's sanctuaries. I was starting to really enjoy the Taizé singing, too, and would experiment by moving around from one singing group to another, looking for where I belonged rather than thinking I didn't belong anywhere. I still don't know for sure what my singing voice is. I seem to be somewhere between tenor and bass, yet I think there is a soprano lurking in there somewhere, waiting to come out. It felt as if I had been away too long from the part of me that could connect with Spirit in this way. Music had always been so powerful in my life, in some ways controlling me. Now I was working creatively with music and allowing song to come from me. It feels great when I know I'm working with Spirit in this way. Nothing ever seems too difficult, and I love the lightness and the joy that the laughter brings.

A few months later, I became friends with a young American woman who was spending some time at Findhorn. She would hang around the lounge some evenings, playing the guitar. I was talking to her about my new relationship with voice and singing. What I wanted to do now was write songs and maybe put some of my poems to music. She started to play her guitar and asked me to sing whatever came from my heart to the music. I did a silent gulp and then thought, no, go for it, Jacqueline. It was such a wonderful experience and I will never be able to thank her enough for helping me achieve a dream. A couple of years ago, I brought a guitar from an Oxfam shop and a friend sorted out some new strings and tuned it for me. I'm looking at it in the corner of the room as I write and am hoping one day to attract someone who will be willing to work with me by bringing the words and the music together.

It would be a year later when I wrote this song as a wish for healing between my mother and me. I say I wrote the song; I was staying at a friend's house, as we were attending a song and dance festival for the weekend, when one morning I woke up and this song wrote itself. My friend came down to see what I was doing at such an unearthly hour and, after glancing at a couple of the verses, he came up with the chorus.

Oh come ye back my mother dear
Now sit ye down at the fire; draw near,
We've ne'er had time to speak these words
Time has come when truth is heard
I appreciate the hurt I felt
It helped my heart to slowly melt
Held a space for me to be free
Helped me search for the truest me.
I learnt to love as never before
'Twasn't you who slammed the door
With anger and my blame as well
If I can love you only time will tell

Chorus
As we reach out to join our hands
We will meet in no one's land
When no one's right and no one's wrong
We've found at last each other's song
We heard the sweetest melody
Where you and I can truly be
Within a place of sweet embrace
Where love at last has shown its face

Oh come ye back my daughter dear
Now sit ye down at the fire; draw near,
I've never said these words before
It broke my heart when you slammed the door
I felt I'd failed my beautiful girl
You were never the shell, always the pearl
I saw the spark, couldn't fan the flame
You were a shrew, not for me to tame
The truest and a shining star
Now you have found the truth you are
I'd always loved you – you couldn't see
'Cause I wasn't being the truest me

Oh come ye closer my mother dear
Now sit ye down at the fire; draw near,

I've never said, 'I missed your touch'
Or that I love you so very much
Words couldn't come – I'd try in vain
To speak my heart – but caught in blame
I thank you for your patient wait
I thank you for the open gate
Thank you just for being you
I know that's all that you could do
I had to be a mother, you see,
Before I knew what it was to be me

Oh come sweet girl to my loving arms
I've always seen your willing charms
The gap between was never real
We put it there so we could heal
We took our sides at the water's edge
The river she froze like a hardened wedge
Trust me now as I throw this line
That everything will turn out fine
In truth, you are already here
There's nothing left for you to fear
Arms extended, heart open wide
There is no need to run or hide

Now here we sit, my mother dear
There's nothing left for us to fear
Our flames are one and growing strong
In unity – share Heaven's song
'Twas why we came to earth this time
I'm blessed to know that all is fine
'Twas love that guided us each day
I now know why I learnt to pray
To heal family was my pact
Now we've found love, no going back
No forgiveness is needed here
We surrendered to love – our pathway's clear

We speak these words so others may hear
No need for us to live in fear
Our voice is one for all to see
Like the birds we're circling free
We soar and share our love around
And as we grow increase the sound
Our voices rise beyond these shores
Heaven's song is becoming yours
For you to choose to become one
With all on Earth, stars, moon and sun

Oh Mother Earth come sit ye here
Share your fire, let us draw near
As we reach out to join our hands
We are meeting in no one's land
Where no one's right and no one's wrong
We've found at last Heaven's earthly song
We are the sweetest melody
Heart open wide – for all to be
Within these arms of sweet embrace
Where we see love in every face.

I was ready now to discard another 'hand-me-down' belief system that I had chosen to hang onto. It was from a musician who gave it to me when I was about twenty. We were part of a group of friends visiting a pub on the Devonshire moors one evening. While we were singing along with others, he whispered in my ear, 'Has anyone ever told you that you are tone deaf?'

Another word, another stone, a different ocean and it was gone. Forgiveness was no longer necessary. I was now recognising the jewels that I had been receiving over my lifetime. I was learning to stand in my power, no longer being a victim or survivor. I was in a place of acceptance – accepting who I was, the person I was becoming to know. Why people had chosen to give me those hand-me-downs was their stuff. From now on, I was going to try to process the lessons that came to me and leave the rest to whoever dealt it.

One of Louise Hay's cards shows a beautiful woman twirling around, saying, 'I am beautiful and everyone loves and appreciates me.' On one occasion at a girlfriend's house, that card came to me three times in a row. She saw the synchronicity and felt that I was supposed to keep the card, so she gave it to me. I carried it around with me for quite a few years and put it up somewhere where I could always see it. It was a reminder of the fear I had of not 'fitting in'. Now from a place of love I am accepted and seen for who I am. I suppose that is a gentle reminder that I can't be accepted for who I am until I know and accept my true self. I have kept the card as a memento and I smile to myself whenever I come across it now. I know that I can't change anyone else; I can only change myself.

The strangest thing was that when I arrived at the Louise Hay workshop for the final day, I couldn't believe that the exercises in store would recreate exactly what had happened in my own front room that morning. It was about reconnecting with the love, just as I had with my ex-partner earlier that day. I took the opportunity to apply the experience to other people in my past, too. It was also important for me to apply the same healing process to myself. Examining the roles that I'd played and the choices I'd made. It was about forgiving myself and through that accepting myself for who I was. I was joyously observing the transformation due to the discovery of the gifts of forgiveness and acceptance.

Going back to my relationship, as it was at that time, was not honouring my journey to find and be my true self. It appeared to be reinforcing my old beliefs, and I noticed that I was making a lot of compromises; I guess my partner was, too. What we ended up with was something that neither of us wanted: a loveless relationship. I can't deny that it was hard to let go of the memories of falling in love with him and what that felt like for many of our years together. What Marianne Williamson says about romantic love in her book *Illuminata – A Return to Prayer* is that 'Falling in love is an effort to retrieve Paradise, that dimension of bliss where no one is blamed for anything and everyone is appreciated for who they are. When we fall in love, we drop, for however brief a time, our tendency to judge. We suspend our disbelief and eschew our faithlessness in another human being.' For that reason alone, I am eternally grateful to him for the part he played in allowing me to connect with that part of me; to know a place I'd never known before and to truly understand the saying that 'it is better to have loved and lost than never to have loved at all'.

It helps me when I read that now to know why I acted the way I did when I stepped out of that place of bliss. It was like entering a type of hell for me – an inner hell. I tried to push down my feelings again, to block them out. I filled my time with work and socialising which involved excessive amounts of alcohol, and it would be some years later before I began the work I wanted to do to face the demons of that time; to look at the hurts I'd inflicted on myself and others and through forgiveness come to an understanding of what had happened and what I had learnt. I came to a state of acceptance – and through that I returned to grace.

This piece of work opened the door for me to look at all the relationship challenges I'd had in my life, particularly the drama around my family and the feelings of not belonging in other places. It also allowed many more of my feelings to surface and to ask for the attention they deserved. However, with my new-found 'tools' of forgiveness and acceptance I felt stronger and knew that when they presented themselves again I would be ready to make the trip.

I have found that being truthful with myself and accepting the whole of me, not just the parts that I want the rest of the world to see or even the parts I want myself to see, is much more fulfilling. Being authentic at any one moment with what some might describe as the light and the dark of my life brings me back to a place of peace. There is always something new coming to light. I'm grateful for the willingness I show in listening to those parts of me and celebrate the transformation that follows. I like to think of the qualities that play out in me at any one time as a pie chart and often ask myself what percentage of the whole is involved. This way, no one voice is overwhelming or consumes me. I've also used this 'tool' when working with others. It's great to see the instant lightness that lifts them when they realise that the part they are not enjoying working with at that moment is only a part of them. It is often a part of them that doesn't usually have as much airtime as the 'nicer' bits of them.

I've found it can be quite useful to have team meetings with myself. Sometimes, before starting the day or when I have a decision to make, I check in with which parts of me want to speak. I ask myself, 'What's alive in me right now?' Not just the parts of me with the loudest voice, either; I allow time for some quieter voices to gain the confidence to speak. When they do, I take it seriously, otherwise they may not speak again and I could lose many golden opportunities.

When I was exploring forgiveness with regard to my then-partner, I felt that scenario represented the ten per cent of the iceberg. What presented itself now was an opportunity to review my life. To go back and visit some of the places I had kept in the dark for most of my life: emotional, mental, physical and sexual abuse – ugliness – suppressed anger – hatred – my attempted suicide – abandonment – grief. All of which manifested in ways such as becoming a victim, a lack of self-worth, self-sabotage, annihilation. As I worked with each of them to their fullness, so I found that space was offered up. This space, it appeared, instantly filled with more love. I noticed that my capacity to love others was greater. I began to love myself and others as I'd never loved them before. Previously, it had been from a place of selflessness. By that, I mean that I had given myself up to please another. From this way of being I discovered that bit by bit I began to disappear until the night I nearly disappeared completely. Now I love from a place I call self; some refer to that as 'being selfish', but to me it was about finding and staying connected to the real self, the real me. The woman I was born to be: a woman who willingly offers herself to others, who exercises her free will and attaches no outcome or expectation to her love. From here there is no victim, no survivor and no aggressor. The circle is broken and the healing creates new opportunities. My free will is now more in line with the line from the Lord's Prayer, 'Thy will be done'. I freely choose to serve, and therefore 'Thy will' is my will.

I have chosen to take personal responsibility for the episodes in my life that have blocked me, such as believing I was unloved or ugly, that I didn't fit in, that I wasn't creative or even that I lacked a singing voice. I also reflect on what comments I might have given to people unwittingly that may have caused such pain, blocks and damage. My prayers have been answered and I know that the damage caused by those words and deeds is not irreparable. As instances come to mind of things I have wished I had not done, I take the opportunity to forgive myself and send love and light to those whom I may have harmed in this way. I suppose in a way this realisation has brought me to a place where I want to be known as a spiritual dreambuilder. I pray each day that I might be connected to the Source in me and see the Source in others. I pray too that I might continue to work with myself and others in building our dreams where we might otherwise be influenced by dreambashers.

What I'm discovering in my life right now is that dreams do become a reality. I am therefore willing to forgive myself for being controlled by fear, to forgive myself for blaming those who I felt fanned the flames of fear and to take responsibility for all of my life, past, present and future.

***** Exercises *****

What are your thoughts and feelings on forgiveness? Allow time for all the voices to be heard. Try not to censor or judge what arises for you; it is your opportunity to hear the truth. Do you notice any differences when exploring forgiveness for others and for yourself?

Forgiveness – write down all the names of those people who have caused you any form of irritation or bad feeling. The length of this list depends on your age and life experience. Take your time and allow your senses to be open to remember those to include. You won't be surprised to find your own name on the list. When you have completed the list, light a candle, align yourself by taking a few deep breaths and then one by one say out loud the person's name and that your intention is to forgive them totally. Let them know that you hold back no unforgiveness. Equally forgive yourself and affirm that you are now both free. You will be surprised that once you have done this exercise, as new irritations occur you will notice it instantly and do a clearing immediately. Alternatively, you might find that doing a review each evening may work for you. Eventually, of course, the hope is you catch it in the thought form and then it gradually disappears as a behaviour pattern.

'Hand-me-downs'/Belief Systems – Can you recall incidents where you have chosen to believe what another said of you? How did it make you feel? Do you still feel that way? How would it feel if that were no longer true? How can you ground this new feeling or self-image so that it becomes a reality? Can you recall incidents which you now regret where you may have given beliefs to another? Would you like to take this opportunity to recompense in some way? How would it feel to know that it was no longer a weight to be carried about by all concerned?

Are you being the real you, the person you were born to be? Is this the real you that you are reflecting to yourself and others? What parts of you have been shaped by others? Sometimes, when we are not living our true self or fulfilling our purpose, it might be because we feel compromised. What/where are you compromising? Is it to do with your relationships, your work, your spirituality, your dreams? What was the dream you came to fulfil? (Don't censor what comes up here, regardless of whether it makes sense or not. The first time I asked the question, I thought I was going to get a job title, and I got 'to bring joy and laughter, through the release of tears'. I can see how that has played out in many things I've been involved in.) Are you honouring that dream? If not, what could you do to start making it a reality?

Do you love yourself? What words describe the person you see looking back at you when you look in a mirror or at a photograph? How deep does the love go? Again, listen to all the voices that want to have a say.

Explore the places where you feel you fit in and where you don't. Why do you think you feel more at ease in some places than in others? What fears may be surfacing when you feel uneasy somewhere? How may you be self-sabotaging or resisting turning up for your dreams? Explore what you might learn if you were to look inward for the answers instead of pointing a finger outward. (Remember, as we point one finger out, we have three pointing back at us.)

Community

A Sense of Belonging

I HAVE ABSOLUTELY NO IDEA WHERE THIS WORD IS LEADING me, but lead me it has done since New Year's Eve, 2001, when it seemed that I knew it for the first time – a time when it was mirrored back to me in a way in which I had not witnessed it before. I'd experienced its joy for a week and it seemed to me as if Source were highlighting its beauty in that magical moment as the sun was setting on a crisp winter's day. It was the end of a year and the end of an era for me. It was a reminder, too, that this was a new beginning. Yet I was also being told that I didn't need a new year to start afresh, or even a new day. I can start anew with every moment and with every breath.

I guess the word 'community' will mean a different thing to each of us. When I looked it up in the Oxford English Dictionary, it said 'joint ownership or common position in regard to something; a body of persons having community of life on any scale (e.g. all members of a state, town, school, convent, profession or beehive)'. The Microsoft thesaurus brought up 'neighbourhood, centre of population, area, district, village, hamlet, commune, society, group of people, kinship, unity, identity, cooperation, cooperative spirit, convergence, meeting, junction, union, similarity'.

For me, 'community' means a meeting of minds, bodies and spirits where each gives willingly and is respected for their gifts and talents and all are able to express and receive as is their need; a place where oneness is reached through the respect of diversity, where we are encouraged and nurtured to be and celebrate our true selves, where we live in gratitude for what we have received and value our environment and all creatures on our planet Earth.

On reflection, it seems that the essence of community has

always been significant to me. What has probably caused me the most pain has been where I have felt the lack of it or the not belonging to it. In my life that could relate to my family, school, church, peer group, college, workplaces, relationships or a geographical place. The interesting thing is that I've never felt out of place geographically. Wherever I've lived in this country or travelled in the world, I have always felt at home. I can remember that from a young age I had a resistance to calling myself English; after all, I had a Yorkshire mother and an Irish father, so I would say that I was 'half English and half Irish'. I then realised that this description didn't take into account where I was born. Later it changed to British, then European, and eventually, when I was asked on my first day at Ruskin College, I answered that I was 'a child of the Universe'. In some way, I'd always felt part of something bigger than I was as an individual, and the community I belonged to was equally limitless. This reminds me of a Hindu Sanskrit greeting I love which is 'namaste'. Roughly translated it means, 'All that is the highest ability, thought, and action in me, greets all that is the highest ability, thought, and action in you. And when you are in that place in you, and I am in that place in me, together we may realise a state of being that is beyond our individual experience of reality and therefore greater than ourselves.' When we acknowledge each other as one, *commune* as one, and connect with something greater than ourselves, we have *unity*. I'm now wondering if that was why I heard the word 'community'.

I'd like to share with you how five different types of community presented themselves to me, following on from that New Year's Eve, and the joys and challenges they brought with them. I've presented only snippets of my experiences, as I'm sure each could be a book in its own right. My hope is that you will get a flavour of the richness that community living has brought me. Maybe you will also see the strands that weave together to create the tapestry of life and healing. It has allowed me the opportunity to grow closer to my true self. It is in this place of self that I am at peace and where I am closer to Source. In so being, I am gradually learning to act from that place within and to witness the Source within others.

Atsitsa – Skyros, Greece

Between leaving my job and going back to study, I felt I would like a couple of weeks in the sun. A girlfriend of mine had told me about her experience in Skyros and it sounded just right for me. For those who haven't been there yet, it is advertised as a holistic holiday experience. In some ways, it's difficult for me to put into words what happened to me there or how it might be for someone else if they went. All I can say is that I had the feeling that I was in the right place at the right time. It is a place where the experiences will continually change depending on the programmes run, the presenters, the director, staff and, of course, the guests who take part. I noticed that it had a strong community opportunity. I say 'opportunity' because no one is conscripted into the programmes if they don't want to take part. There are plenty of options to work, play and learn together or not. How it best serves you is up to you.

Skyros has two venues on the island and you can choose to stay in its town or beach venue. I was drawn to the beach venue but opted to stay in the one large house there, rather than the thatched huts. In truth, I suppose if there is a 'five-star hotel' versus 'camping' option going on then I'm drawn to 'five-star'. Don't get me wrong; I'm not saying that the house at Atsitsa would be rated as five-star in a hotel brochure, but compared to the huts that was what it represented to me at the time.

I enjoyed the whole fortnight, even though at times I would be crying my eyes out. I had begun to value my need to cry. I'd spent years telling others and myself that they wouldn't see me cry. It was the way I dealt with the pain. I remember that only a few months before going to Skyros that I told a friend I was holding a lot of tears inside me. When he asked me how many, I told him six weeks' worth. That was a lot of tears, I realised, and I made a pact with myself not to stop them coming any more. I also appreciate that when something is repressed it often acts out inappropriately, like crying in front of my boss because something had been triggered inside me that I hadn't previously processed. I needed to spend time with myself to give permission for my tears to surface. I had no way of knowing that Skyros was going to be that loving space which allowed them to flow. I will always be grateful to her for offering herself up in that way.

It was a couple of years later before I was to understand that it wasn't just my tears that needed attention. I also needed time and space to access and process my grief, anger and love. I wanted to have access to all my feelings. I wanted them back. This was not something that happened overnight; it is a gentle ongoing process, and I'm grateful for the opportunity to work with my feelings in 'bite-size' pieces. I have in the past attended counselling sessions and workshops to process these issues, but, although they went part of the way towards my healing process, it seemed to me that there was a part that I needed to work with myself. When I found this, I discovered a way of life and my spiritual 'tool kit'. When I began working with what I call my inner child, my 'little Jackie' helped release some of the tears and also allowed me to have an ongoing relationship with her. I honoured our connection on the island by writing my first ever poem, which I called 'Postcard to Myself'. It seemed as if I was now able to give her time to have the attention she so richly deserved. By the end of the holiday I had written a second poem, called the 'Beauty of Atsitsa', which was a synopsis of my experience on the island; a poem of acknowledgement of what I had received. Creativity was stifled in me quite early on, so producing a piece of work such as a poem was very rewarding for me. However, what arose from creativity was the fear of sharing it.

At the end of the fortnight, there was a gathering where people were invited to take part in whatever way they wanted. There were opportunities to do this collectively or individually. Some people played instruments, sang songs or put sketches together. Although I was part of the drumming group that was going to perform, I noticed that this wasn't a real challenge to me. The real fear would be going out on stage, on my own, offering up my own work. I so much wanted to do that, yet I shrank from the fear of opening myself up to that. To be exposed in such a way, to offer up my vulnerability: it all felt too scary for me. Whereas hidden within a group of drummers – that was nothing. I have to say that the inspiration to work through this fear came from a book I'd taken with me. It was *Billy* by Pamela Stephenson. I found it a very moving book. I'd always been a fan of Billy Connelly, because he seemed to have a gift to share social issues through humour. I've never seen him live, but when I watched his TV performances or videos he was always able to lift my spirits. The telling of his story inspired me to take things lightly and to look for the humorous side of situations. Not in a belittling way, but more in a way to move beyond. I also read that he was often 's—t scared' just before he went on stage. Remembering this helped me put myself forward to share my poem. I thought that if Billy could do it after all the experiences in his life, so could I. I was really nervous backstage, waiting to go on, but as soon as the lights dimmed I walked on stage, took my seat and the fear evaporated. I began to feel at ease, even comfortable with being there, and what was important now was releasing my poem. I remember feeling that the response to my poem was secondary to the lightness and freedom I was now feeling, compared to the fear which had previously gripped me. I'd like to share that poem with you now.

Postcard to Myself

I wish I could have held you tight to show you that I
  cared.
I wish I could have kissed your face and combed your
  curly hair.
I wish I could have been there to protect you from all
  harm.
I wish I'd tucked you up in bed to keep you safe and
  warm.
I wish I could have told you that you were the
  shiniest star.
I wish I could have told you how beautiful you are.
I would have tried to protect your ears from your
  parents' shouting fights.
Especially when the windows broke and you worried
  through the nights.
I remember you being excited when you went off to
  your school.

You thought you might be liked and loved but alas
they were also cruel.
They held your nose to make you drink. They hit you
with a rule.
When you couldn't pick it up as quick you were made
to feel the fool.
I wish I could have been with you for your wounds
I'd surely lick.
I'd tell them to treat kids like that is well and truly
sick.
I wish I could have been with you when you ran
away.
'Please don't go, I love you so,' I could have helped
her say.
I wish I could have been with you when you arrived
at your boyfriend's place.
With my help we could have convinced him that you
needed your own space.
But alas that didn't happen and again the silent cries
came.
Now listen to me, little one, you are definitely not to
blame.
I wish I could have been with you on your wedding
day.
'You can change your mind, it's not too late,' I could
have helped him say.
I wish I could have been with you as the turbulent
years rolled by.
I wish I could have been your voice instead of your
silent cry.
I wish I could have dispersed the pain and licked your
flowing tears.
I wish you had not been alone inside those silent
fears.
So I'm sorry, my little one, that I wasn't there for you.
But now it's said and you feel safe. I feel beautifully
anew.

There's more to tell you, darling, and when the time
is right,
I'll hold your hand and hug you close when we visit
those dark silent nights.
So remember this, my little one: as sure as night turns
into day,
You will never be alone again because in my arms
you'll stay.

Later on in the evening, people sought me out and told me how moving my poem was and how much it had touched their lives. One person even said I ought to send it to social services, as they thought it might be helpful for children to hear it. I was already pleased to have had the experience and I was now more pleased that in serving myself, I had also served others.

At Skyros, putting on the production was definitely a community event, as were the mealtimes. Although there were staff to organise the meals and keep the site tidy, guests were given the opportunity to help out for about twenty minutes each day. They could help by preparing vegetables, setting up tables or sweeping the communal areas. It was a lovely feeling being part of this and often a song or two would be sung. There were opportunities to meet up in family groups, too; these were called Ekos. We would gather for about half an hour a day to share what was going on for us. Being part of sharing groups and circles has played a big part in my life since then. I believe it is really important to have group times whatever the size and structure: be it families, workplaces or with like-hearted people. We also had the opportunity to meet up with someone on a daily basis to experience co-listening. This was interesting, as I think co-listening is great but I can see that for some people it can be quite challenging: especially for those who want to fix things, rescue people or sort you out. Instead, the intention is to give the person sharing an opportunity to hear their words repeated back without judgement, advice or any non-verbal reflections. I know that when I have had something reflected back to me in that way it has been quite revealing. At times, it grounds something for me, and on other occasions it allows me to question it. Sometimes, it is as if I have heard it for the first time. To begin with, I was fearful of not being able to remember everything that had been said. People were encouraged to talk for about fifteen minutes uninterrupted. Then you would reflect back, in their words, what they had said. I decided that all I could do was my very best. I also discovered that when I was listening from the heart and not expected to think of a response, I had more space free to hold what they said.

The fortnight allowed time for people to get to know each other and to experience a sense of community. We worked, socialised, ate and played together. For me, it was a very supportive environment, and I was grateful to the staff who worked so caringly and lovingly to hold a space for us to be and to transform in. Among many things, I was reconnected with my inner child, my creativity, my beauty and a sense of family and had the opportunity to have a love affair with a twenty-six foot yacht. I particularly enjoyed the early morning walking meditations, and I received many gifts on those occasions. The one that particularly comes to mind is the difference between walking forwards and backwards. The roads and tracks were unmade and often dotted with potholes of varying sizes. Our guide would ask us to follow him on these walks, and when he turned to walk backwards, we would, too. The interesting thing was that I only tripped in the potholes when I was walking forwards. What I learnt from that was that when I walked backwards, I put my trust in God that no harm would come to me, and it never did. When I walked forwards, I didn't do that; I was looking for the danger points, and guess what? I found them.

As I've said, many tears rolled during those two weeks, and there were many smiles, too. I released some hardened shells and welcomed the new vulnerable me. I discovered that my vulnerability was my strength.

Now it was time to go home and release the last few items of furniture from my house before setting off for my new halls of residence in Oxford. Would you believe that one of the last things to go was a dishwasher? I thought that would have been the first to go. There I was, washing up in Atsitsa, when the guy standing next to me at the sinks stepped on my toe. We started talking and I mentioned that here we were, washing up, and I had a perfectly good dishwasher at home that I was trying to release before I moved.

'Really?' he said. 'I could do with one of them.'

'Well, if you live near Reading and can pick it up within a few days after you get back, it's yours.'

He smiled as he told me he lived five miles away from me and would be over on the Monday night. Another coincidence: out of the fifty guests there that fortnight, I met another four from Reading. Not only that; one worked for the same company as my ex, and I only realised that as I recognised someone she was talking about who worked with him. They say it's a small world and we never have to go more than six people removed before there is a connection.

This next poem is offered in gratitude to the island of Atsitsa and to all those I met during the two weeks I was there.

Atsitsa

The beauty of Atsitsa, where do I really start?
Oh, yes, I remember the delicious pear tart.
Silent meditative walks, with poignant thoughts for
  the day.
Courses to attend and 'Trost', a new word for me to
  say.
Learning massage techniques. Being watched by
  caring eyes,
Afternoons spent sailing under glorious blue skies.
New friends gained daily and a family called Ekos
  too.
Then the tears and pain would come and wash all
  over you.
I remember the day I lost my shell, it was gone when
  I awoke.
I was left feeling vulnerable, uncovered, fearful of
  being broke.
I cried as if it wouldn't stop. I sat and looked out to
  sea,

A friend came back, placed his hand on my shoulder
and quietly spoke to me.
I explained how I was truly shaken to discover I had
no shell.
He told me it had disintegrated because I'd outgrown
it full and well.
I told how I had envisaged birds flying over the
vulnerable, fleshy me.
He suggested that instead of eating me alive, their
wings from the sun shielded me.
As one day turned into two, I became stronger and
more alive.
The world seemed a different place now – one in
which I would thrive.

Ruskin College, Oxford, England

Two weeks after arriving home from Atsitsa, I was to arrive at Ruskin, filled with wonderment of what might unfold. Not just the opportunity to experience academic learning at a higher level than I had before, but also to do so without fear of previous experiences. The sense of community I got while studying at Ruskin College in 2002/2003 was powerful beyond my imagination. Obviously, having chosen to give up my home and live in halls, I was expecting some form of communal living, but what I experienced surpassed all expectations. We were constantly being told that we were an exceptional year, and I wondered if they told every year that because in some way it would be true. However, friends I studied with who stayed on after I left have said that it was true and no years since have matched it for them. I remember sitting in our lecture rooms, looking around at the faces and thinking, why this year? Why have we as individuals been brought together this year? Not last year or next year, but this year.

There were some pretty special people there that year, as students, lecturers, counsellors, librarians, administrators or guests. They were constantly blowing my mind away with their endless giving, hope, support, kindness, growth, vulnerability, courage, love, understanding and truth. Surrounded by that, we had an opportunity not to shy away from our fears, disagreements, frustrations, isolation and all the so-called 'baggage' we brought with us.

The college is on two sites and it was interesting to see the people who were drawn to live at the respective halls. There is the Walton Street site in the centre of Oxford, where the college first opened a century ago. This was mainly for the 'townies', it seemed, whereas the 'country bumpkins', of which I was one, gravitated to the Headington site, about four miles from the city centre. It wasn't exactly in the country, but the house was very old and had probably at one time been a 'country house'. The house has substantial grounds and within it has purpose-built accommodation for the students. We studied at both, so were able to get the best of both worlds, which pleased me. It was amazing how clear people were about which site they wanted to live on. Maybe I had been used to grander living in a previous life, but I knew I wanted to live in the 'big house', and I was one of the six students who were able to live there. We were the last to do so. All the students on that site now live in the modern blocks.

One of the decisions I'd made before going there to study was that I would not get involved in the politics. I'd just spent the last five or six years being involved in both managerial and union positions. I've always been one of those people who wanted to get involved – to be active in the community and to ensure there was justice. I was happy in both roles and did not feel any conflict when swapping hats. In fact, for me it was useful to be able to see something from another perspective when debating issues. My hope was that many things would be ironed out before they became deadlocked. During my working and private life, I seemed to have gravitated towards focus groups, often representing marginalised people, departments or organisations at many different levels. The idea about not getting involved in Ruskin politics was because I wanted to really give my studying a chance. I'd waited many years to get there and I'd given up a lot. I wanted to give this opportunity my best shot, and I wasn't sure how much of me it would need. This was when I realised that the Universe does not understand the word 'not'. Since then, when putting a request out there, I have only concentrated on the positive aspect of what I want answered or manifested. When I've heard myself include the word 'not' I've quickly scrambled to get it back and erase it. On this occasion, it was too late, and I think maybe it was therefore meant to be.

It was while we were being addressed by two students from the previous year, who were organising a meeting to set up the Student Union, that a thought seemed to come in from nowhere. The thought was for me to stand as the president of the Student Union. Incidentally, I've noticed thoughts like that popping in a lot more since I chose to listen that time.

'No, please don't ask me to do that,' I uttered internally.

'Oh, yes,' was the clear answer I heard back. Although I had got involved in things in the past, I wasn't the one who usually put myself forward, and definitely not for something like President. My fears, of course, would be of rejection, feeling foolish, not being picked, not being up to the job or even the thought that I would be putting myself above my station. Where do those 'hand-me-downs' come from? Thank God I didn't know what was involved, or I might have used my free will to decline. Knowing hardly anyone there – we were only in the first week of the term – I approached a couple of students who were sitting in front of me. I had briefly met them when attending a familiarisation week held in the summer recess. They seemed to think it was a great idea for me to stand and said they would be willing to nominate me. During the break, I was also approached independently by a couple of other students who had heard me speak at the meeting and asked if I would stand for President. OK, I thought, I guess this is what I'm supposed to be doing. So, if that's the case, I'm going to need the help of the angels to work with me. I had connected with angels earlier on in the year and I now wanted to experiment with working with them in this capacity. I have no idea what my fellow student executives would have felt if I had shared that with them.

Once elected, I decided that I would ask the angels to work with me in this role. I wanted to experiment with working with them to achieve the highest good for all. Also, a part of me believed that they might have been the ones responsible for getting me into this situation. I often wonder what my fellow students, the principal or the Board of Governors would have thought if they had known I would meditate before each meeting and ask my angels and guides to be present. By working this way, I began to have more trust in myself than ever before. It was the first time I remember feeling guided, that this was what I was supposed to be doing. This helped me out on many occasions.

It was a challenging year. The first of the two main issues that year was the proposal to sell the two college sites. This felt like selling off our heritage. The second was the onset of the war in Iraq. Despite the challenges I was grateful for the opportunities that being President gave me. It meant I got to meet and work with many of the students and faculty and was happy to be an elected representative working with Spirit. I tried very hard to work with everyone, especially those who it seemed were on the opposite side. Some could see that, and others just saw the enemy. Yet I did learn to trust my intuition, and many things that I picked up energetically played out during that year.

What I enjoyed most about the community was the diversity. We were from different backgrounds, countries, cultures, and our age range went from twenty to those in their seventies. Some students had brought their children to live with them, and we all supported each other the best way we could. It was a wonderful example of people asking for what they needed and someone coming forward to help. It seemed as if we had a wealth of talents among us and people were happy to share and give of them freely. We were fed by the college during the week, but at weekends it was down to us. There would always be a communal meal being organised somewhere. Most of us, it seemed, had found our niche, and it appeared there was a lot of acceptance around that and very little comparing of who did what or who didn't.

The students organised some great social evenings, too, such as turning the common room into the 'pink giraffe cocktail lounge' and then a few weeks later into a reggae venue. Not forgetting, of course, the end-of-year Red Ball. There were poetry evenings, musical sharings, children's parties (organised by some of the young students who didn't have children for the students who did). We saw our youngest child there turn one and take his first steps, had a couple of students get married and others who got engaged. We also had some divorces and, sadly, two of our fellow students died. It seemed as if we were a microcosm of the world with all its challenges, joys, pains, addictions, celebrations. We had warmongers, peacemakers and, quite markedly, some of the greatest transformations. All the qualities and events being reflected in our community were all those that were happening in the world beyond.

Some students achieved remarkable grades beyond their wildest dreams, and those who needed help were always supported, whether it was with their studies or other life situations. I know I was blessed to go there and have the experience of that community when I did. Fellow students often come into my thoughts, and on occasions we will meet up and catch up with who is doing what and who has heard from whom. Sadly, the last time I returned to the college was to remember one of my creative writing tutors who had passed away. He was one of the truest representations of a community person you could meet: an inspirational man, a mentor, caring, nurturing; he always seemed to understand where you came from, had a wonderful sense of humour and carried his illness with dignity, as he had his life in the year that I studied with him.

I made a conscious decision when I arrived, which was that I was going to be the 'real' me. With what I had been experiencing recently, I suppose I had begun to realise that I'd hidden a lot of who I was, mainly because I hadn't discovered her before. Somewhere along the journey, I had decided that I was unlovable and unworthy. I'd gone through quite an awakening the year before I arrived at Ruskin. Firstly with the Louise Hay course, learning to love myself and heal my life, and then with a course based on the book by Nick Williams, *The Work We Were Born to Do*. This second course was run by a local man who had called it 'Do the Work You Love – Love the Work You Do'. I instantly expanded the essence of that for myself and included, 'Live the Life You Love – Love the Life You Live'. I had become a colourful, vibrant bird who was happy to show her colours. I no longer wanted to shrink as a reaction. I had started to become comfortable with the newly awoken me. So much so that, when asked at a 'get to know you evening', 'If you could be anybody in the world, living or dead, who would you choose to be?':

'Me. I choose to be me. Jacqueline Iris Daly.'

It was wonderful to know that and feel it vibrate through my body. I think it might have sounded corny or crass to some of those around, me but I wasn't going to change it. They just didn't know my story. That didn't mean I wanted to evangelise in any way, but I wanted to reflect who I truly was, which would also include my spirituality. Can you believe it: on the first evening when we were gathered in the common room, meeting for the first time, I'd brought angels into the conversation and the guy to my left started talking about ones he'd seen and his psychic experiences? Then the woman opposite chipped in with her near-death and out-of-body experience. That year, spirituality was alive in some of our lives, as normally as anything else that was important to us.

What I learnt from that experience was that when we think we are alone with our beliefs, we are alone. When we are brave enough to be our true selves, it can allow others the opportunity to be themselves, too. That year was also a wonderful opportunity to meet people who were truly working with identifying themselves.

We had come together as disparate people and, at the end of a year studying together, left as family members whose time had come to leave home. Despite our diversity, there was a thread that wove between us, stronger than anyone could break. A long time ago we had all said 'yes' to turning up that year, to studying together, to being the community we had become and to being part of the countless learnings and transformations which unfolded that year and continue to do so.

I felt that the Ruskin community experience enriched me with many treasures: an exam which I passed with distinction, an opportunity to be a leader who worked with spirit, people whom I can now call my friends, the inspiration to one day write a book and have it published, expansion of my comfort zones and a deeper understanding of the person I was born to be. It was also the place where I noticed trees for the first time in my life. I know that sounds strange, but it is true. They caught my eye wherever I went, and I often wondered why. I heard it said that within the city of Oxford, no matter where you are, it is always possible to look up and see a tree.

When I packed up my car for the last time, it was with gratitude that I took a final look at the college. The place I had called home for the past year. I was beginning to be comfortable with leaving somewhere because of natural progression, rather than leaving it with a slamming door, as I had done as a seventeen-year-old. Leaving or releasing was taking on a new dimension for me. It had become a positive rather than a negative. It was time for me to move on for further learning and transformation.

Studying at Ruskin was the first tick on my new to-do list. My dreams were becoming reality. It seemed no wonder to me that as a child of seventeen I would have ached for an experience such as this. Writing a book would bring another dream into a reality. I was remembering the visualisation I had where I saw my hand rest on the book I had written. Studying creative writing that year had taught me so much. It taught me how hungry I was to learn, to expand. It also taught me how much I wanted to write, just as I had as a child before it was dashed. I remembered one of the tutorials when I was expressing my frustration about appearing to have a block with regard to my poetry. My tutor just looked at me, telling me that it would all come in its own good time. I wonder if when he said those words he could have known that within an hour of my leaving his rooms a poem would be writing itself in my head. However, I was on a crowded bus and couldn't locate my pen and paper, which were at the bottom of my rucksack. I kept praying as the lines unfolded that I would remember it until I got back to my study room. When the bus pulled up at my stop, I ran all the way back to the halls, praying that I would see no one who needed to talk to me. I kept my eyes to the ground and ran up the stairs, unlocking the door to my room. Threw my rucksack on the bed and switched on the computer and out she came. It called itself...

My Queendom

My home it is a palace in which I am truly Queen.
The fight for freedom now secured is all so plainly seen.
The walls scream out with liberty, free spirit and success.
The time has come when being me is what I do the best.
Nor more I live another script writ for someone who's not me.
I live within my Queendom, a land where I am truly free.
Upon my head I wear a crown so light I can hardly feel.
No burdens now to weigh me down; it all feels too surreal.
Yet in my heart I know it's true, I've reached my launching pad.
Although the journey has seemed long and cruel, I'm happy, no longer sad.
The orb I carry in my hand reflects the work I need to do.
It is the duty in my land to ensure I see it through.
No more the callous world for me where people count as nowt.
My words will reflect for all to see what I am all about.
The cloak of wisdom that I wear stretches far beyond my land.
The path I take is not so rare; it's easy to understand.
Especially when you know it was a gift that came to me.
My palace and my Queendom were born from the love of me.

As I neared the end of my year, I had a conversation with the Dean about where I would go next to study. I knew I wanted to carry on my self-development but, wherever I looked, nothing spoke to me.

Nothing attracted me. As I walked away from the meeting, it dawned on me that my future had already been written.

My mind went back more than a year. At that point, I was still in Reading, helping a friend. She ran an organisation called Life Times. Her guest that day was to be William Bloom, talking about endorphins. I had never heard of him or endorphins, yet found myself drawn to the workshop. By now, I was starting to pay attention to what drew me, especially if I had no logical explanation for it.

I enjoyed helping my friend to set the place up for the event, and when I was asked to help William sell his books during the lunch break I was more than happy to do so. He is a remarkable person, who thankfully spoke in a language I could easily understand. He was also very friendly and we got talking. He asked me about myself and I explained my wish to give up my job in IT, to do some studying and maybe something a bit more 'holistic' with my life. Although I didn't know exactly what 'holistic' would look like, I remember it was the word I used. Another thought that came into my consciousness around that time was related to work. I was thinking that I might not be ready to be put out to pasture when I was sixty-five. If I remained an employee, I would be governed by that rule. Having been a single mother for most of my children's lives, I'd had very little spare money to invest in a pension fund. Therefore, the question running around my head at the time was: what would I be able to turn my hand to when I retired in order to support myself? What I wanted, I suppose, was to be in control. To be creative about how my work might look. I had this sense that I wanted my life and my work to be the same. I didn't want to have different hats or faces to present to people. I had been to a workshop presented by Barbara Winter entitled 'Making a Living Without a Job'. How empowering that was. To be able to choose what hours of the day you worked – maybe even what seasons of the year. Also, working from home had been something I really wanted to do. That desire hadn't gone away, since I wanted to be at home to look after my babies. At that time, though, I had attracted situations that took me away from them.

While skimming through William's book, I discovered another

word I didn't understand. That word was 'Findhorn'. So I asked him what it meant. After all, I hadn't heard of endorphins before today, so maybe 'Findhorn' was a word relating to something similar. With a wry smile, he explained it was a place. I remember being thrown by that, but he went on to clarify that it was a holistic community. After hearing what I'd said earlier, he suggested it might be a place I'd like to try.

'But what is it like?' I asked him.

Another smile. 'It's a different experience for everyone,' he said. 'Maybe you should check it out.'

Apparently, he had lived there himself for a while. The lunch break was over and the event continued, but I vowed I'd do some research and look this place up on the Internet.

At home that evening, I picked up the book I was reading: *A Little Light on Angels*, by Diane Cooper, which I noticed was published by Findhorn Press. Wow, what a coincidence, I thought. I recognise it as synchronicity these days and definitely notice it when something happens three times. Within a few days I picked up another book, also published by Findhorn Press. That was the research over, as far as I was concerned. I was going. I telephoned them and was able to book onto the Experience Week Programme they were running, which coincided with my Christmas holidays from Ruskin. It was strange that even before I went to Findhorn, when I was in one of my creative writing classes, we were asked to write the back cover of what we imagined would be our first book. I wrote among other things that I would spend a year living in Findhorn. How did I know I was going to spend a year there? I hadn't even had my first visit then! But a year it was. During the February break at Ruskin and then the Easter one, I attended further courses. This prepared me to enrol on the three-month Foundation Programme when my academic year at Ruskin came to an end.

Findhorn Foundation, Morayshire, Scotland

Living in and being part of that community was a wonderful experience, and I truly understood what William had meant when he said that it was different for everyone who went there. It really was a mystery school. I saw it myself, both as a student and then as one who worked with the Findhorn guests. Everyone had a different journey. Everyone brought and received different gifts, even if some of them were not always recognisable at the time.

As a student there, I had the opportunity to process many things and at times experience some pain and cry more tears. I suppose I would liken it to 'growing pains'. I really was awake and, as with Ruskin, I wanted to get the fullest experience I could. I'd given up my home and my job and had done so because I felt that this was the best way for me to learn. I could have carried on working full time, living the way I was, going on courses and developing in that way, but I knew it would take me anything from ten to fifteen years. I decided to give it my full attention. I was definitely here to learn. The three-month programme was excellent and I would highly recommend it. I guess that like anything else at Findhorn, no two programmes would ever be the same, so it would be hard to describe it in general terms to anyone. What I would say, though, is that I believe I got the opportunity to learn the lessons I needed to learn. There were opportunities to share my gifts and talents, too. Again, I was like a kid in a sweet shop. There was so much on offer, and I was open to experience not just the programme I was on but the community itself, with all its offerings. The people who touched my life there would be too numerous to mention. Some, who were my facilitators and mentors, will know who they are. Others whom I met and have remained friends with, regardless of where we all are geographically, they will know who they are. There will be others, I guess, who will never know how much they touched my life. It may have been with a word, a smile, a tear, a story, a hug or a trigger. Just as I imagine I will not always know whose lives I have touched.

Again, like Skyros and Ruskin before it, this community is on two sites: Cluny and the Park, as they are colloquially known. Throughout my times at Findhorn, I would always live at Cluny and be drawn to spend time in the Park. I felt at home at Cluny College from the moment I entered its doors for the first time. I was a bit late for the start of the programme because when I was checking on flights I had the option of being a day early or an hour late. After checking with my angels, I chose an hour late. A choice I realised I would never have made before. I felt comfortable with it, too. Guess my surprise when I was working in the kitchen in Cluny that week and the focaliser said something along the lines that Findhorn is the place to play with doing something in a way you don't normally do. The example given was that if you normally worked fast you could try working slowly or vice versa. Great, I thought, so it was fine arriving late when normally I would have turned up a day early and incurred the extra cost.

In some ways, it still feels like home to me. A home I have often returned to, and I shall continue to do so. Sometimes to catch up with the family and to experience what makes my heart sing: the connection, respect, diversity, oneness, love, fun, laughter, community, song, dance, stillness, rapture, depth and lightness. The Phoenix shop, sanctuaries, hot tub, northern lights, Taizé singing, 5Rhythms, sacred dance, café, Cluny Unplugged, trance dance, spiritual support groups, Burns Night, Erraid, Iona, non-violent communication, creative expression, a Course in Miracles, weddings, naming ceremonies, passings, festivals, shamanic journeys, Devas, angels, Cullurne Gardens, prayer, film nights, gatherings, and so I could go on. Of course, outside the Foundation's two main sites there was the beauty of Scotland itself with all its breathtaking sunrises and sunsets, snow-topped mountains and lush green valleys. In Scotland you are never far from water, whether it is the ruggedness of smashing waves, cascading waterfalls, rushing rivers, meandering streams or mirrored lochs. To me, both Findhorn and Scotland were paradise. Before I went there, I'd heard that it always rained in Scotland and that you would be eaten alive by midges. For the year I was there, I hardly noticed the rain and never saw any midges, let alone being bitten by one. I did however notice the friendliness of its people; the vast open spaces; more colours on a hillside than there are in a multitude of rainbows; more trees, woods and mountains than I'd ever seen in my life before, and experiences that will serve me for the rest of my life.

Even though most guests paid for their courses, there were some bursaries. All programmes had sessions slotted into them to allow guests the experience of working within the community. It is an important part of the programme, and the feedback given suggests that for most people it was very rewarding. I was able to receive a fuller experience of community life, learn a different way of working and find I was able to integrate my inner and outer work. How many opportunities does one get to connect with the essence of unconditional love and the Christ energy while cleaning a toilet? When I became a member of the community, the majority of my time was spent in one of the work departments. Working is colloquially known as 'Work as Love in Action', and it truly is. Whether I was preparing a meal, organising and cleaning the communal spaces, gardening, maintaining the buildings and sites or growing food, it was all offered from a place of love. When I worked from that place the food would taste sumptuous, the plants and vegetables would flourish, the rooms would sparkle and everybody would notice the care that was taken over the environment. I could write a book about those experiences alone, and no doubt throughout this one I will refer back to my stay there. Findhorn offered me the opportunity to explore my spirituality in my own way, at my own speed. It held a space for me to nurture it and gradually to integrate it into my being. It taught me how to creatively express it in my channelled poetry.

Through everything that was being presented to me externally, I was learning to find my own inner wisdom. A place where I learnt to trust what was a truth for me. I believe there are often many truths. Mine may appear different from another's, but it doesn't mean that one is wrong and the other right. Knowing this has enabled me to stand in my power and not to be intimidated by others standing in theirs. I have learnt to live my life in gratitude and noticed the difference that it brings. I've learnt to notice what I resist. Gratitude was one of those things. I would have said that I was a pretty grateful person, but what Findhorn did was give me an opportunity to feel and know gratitude more fully. I can remember being really irritated by one person. I thought she was great in every way, except for one thing which really irked me. I couldn't understand the intensity of this feeling. It seemed that every time we shared, which you do a lot of at Findhorn, she wanted to express how grateful she was. So much so, it seemed to me, that when it got to her time to share I would begin to cringe at the thought of what she was going to be grateful for next and start looking around for a 'sick bucket'. It did occur to me, though, that I might be missing an opportunity here. So I worked on releasing my blocks and opening my heart to what she was saying. When I did, I completely understood where she was coming from. I think maybe I'd been told in the past that I was an ungrateful child and therefore this particular incident triggered the negativity in me and I needed to deal with that before I could see the gift I was getting. Oh, I love it now when I feel that way. I've begun to recognise it as an opportunity to experience a great shift within me. The greater the resistance, the nearer to my divine path I've discovered it is possible for me to become.

There is a thought that whatever we see in another that aggravates, irritates or angers us is an invitation to look at the part of us that we are unhappy about, a part which is yet to be healed. Some people are horrified at this thought: that when angered by an abuser they may have an abuser in them, or an aggressor or a victim. My truth is that we are made up of the whole. All of us are everything and our time here is an opportunity to heal all the parts of us. Sometimes by healing ourselves we can help to heal others. I believe therefore that there will be traits of an aggressor in me, an abuser, a victim, a hero, a saint, etc. Now, if I have a negative reaction to something, I take it as an opportunity to heal. An opportunity to connect with that part of me that wishes to return to love. For those qualities and behaviours to be expressed from a loving place. For instance, when we look at an aggressor, instead of seeing the negative, we can look at the attributes of an aggressor and see what the positives might be. They are often focused, achieve what they want and are connected to their power, to name just a few. To deny the aggressor in us is to deny all of these qualities. Therefore, the suggestion is to harness the qualities and heal the behaviour attached to them. So when something we don't like the look of is reflected back to us, the invitation is not to deny it but to look at where that behaviour is now or where it has played out in our lives. Allow it to be seen so that it can be healed. Know it as a blessing, not a curse.

I always end my day before sleep listing the things in my life that I am particularly grateful for. Some will be linked to the experiences of the day, such as life events, conversations, interactions, gifts, and others will be things that I could take for granted, like thanking the parts of my body that work so hard every day to support my soul's journey, the sun for rising, the rain for falling, people for smiling. I always bless my food and water and give thanks to the beings seen and unseen that have brought them to my table and to Mother Earth for continually sustaining me. When I shower or bathe, I like to caress my body, to appreciate it for its beauty and, of course, for the beauty of the planet and Universe. As I do this, I often send blessings to the person who irritated me enough to bring the true essence of gratitude into my life and make me look for the potential learning in all the irritations I feel.

Another irritation occurred during the three-month Foundation Programme when I knew we were going to be spending half a day on prayer. I had looked at the programme and thought it was all brilliant except for this slot on prayer. I don't do this religious stuff, I remember thinking; not all this down on your knees and praying for forgiveness. Again, I think this must have triggered something from my childhood. As I've already mentioned, I attended a Roman Catholic school, and it seemed that I'd accumulated, according to the adults around me, a lot of sin that I didn't think belonged to me. To put it all right often seemed to include a lot of praying, some of which was in Latin that meant absolutely nothing to me. I also witnessed that a lot of these people who were obviously doing a lot of praying didn't seem to be particularly kind to each other or to children. However, I was in for the whole event, so along I went to the prayer session, willing myself to be open-minded. The guy who was going to lead the session walked in and all my judgements and projections came flooding to the forefront. He definitely looked like one of those praying sorts of guys. Thankfully, I had learnt to 'witness myself' and observe that I was operating in a way that no longer served me. Releasing my judgement, I opened my heart. To say I was blown away is an understatement. What he had to share was so powerful for me. It started with the way he opened the session. It might seem very ordinary printed on a page, but I can highly recommend using it when you are part of any group. I often use it myself and always receive feedback of its powerfully connecting energy.

We were asked to follow his lead and repeat what he said. One by one we said our names together with a request 'please take a breath with me', so when it was my turn I said, 'My name is Jacqueline; please take a breath with me.' There would be a short pause before the next person spoke and so it would continue until all twenty of us had taken part. Simple, I know, but the power that was generated as we slowly went around the room was literally breathtaking, if you'll excuse the pun. We had created a space of oneness. We had all offered up ourselves by the speaking of our name. We had made a request to everyone to share the breath and all had said yes. We were sharing the same air. We were breathing as one.

Then he shared his story of his connection with prayer with us. He gave us examples of prayer which were like nothing I'd ever witnessed before. They appeared to me to be creative expressions of life, and the invitation was that I could make up my own. I remember thinking 'that fits into my belief system'. A few weeks later, synchronistically, I was introduced to a book called *Illuminata – A Return to Prayer* by Marianne Williamson. It was a 'national one bestseller' in the States and I couldn't put it down, much like the other books written by her that I've read since. That was it; I was off, writing my own prayers and allowing what wanted to be said to come through. This was when I started to add prayer to my daily life. It seemed a great way for me to converse with Source, and the silence I held afterwards was a great way for me to receive messages back. Little did I know then that eighteen months later I would be living in Reading and reaching out to my community with a dialogue entitled 'Prayer – a modern-day tool for peaceful living'. Not only was I to have that experience, but I was also invited onto the local radio station to discuss the topic with a wider audience.

Life wasn't all roses at Findhorn. Some issues that arose failed to be healed during the time that I spent there. I wasn't disappointed, though; I knew what these were, and I invited them to present themselves again in another situation or community so that I could get the opportunity to heal from them. Sometimes, flogging a dead horse is not the way to go.

With all that I experienced there, I only have to think the word 'Findhorn' and its essence fills my body and soul. Beautiful faces come to mind and the feeling swells. When I feel that way, it always seems to ripple out around the globe and I connect with the people who have passed through the community and are now back home. I like to imagine that maybe they are thinking beautiful thoughts, too. So I can visualise the whole planet and its people receiving love because of Findhorn being there and holding the space that it does by contributing its work. Not only for the guests it attracts, but for all the organisations that have sprung up from within it and for all the outreach work it is involved in.

Eventually, I felt it was time to leave the community. I had no idea where I was to go next. As that was the case, I didn't mention it to anyone for a couple of weeks and just sat with it. Then I realised that I had to say I was going in order for something new to come in. I was working in Cluny kitchen at the time, and as we were checking in with each other before the shift I mentioned that I felt it was time for me to leave. During the shift, I got the obvious question:

'Where are you going?'

Of course at that time I didn't have an answer, except that I thought it would be made known to me. Two hours later, someone I hardly knew happened to be on the shift. She said she felt she ought to share some information with me. She told me about a woman in Croatia who was hoping to do an exchange with someone in Findhorn. To cut a long story short, four weeks later I was off to the island of Krk in Croatia. The strange thing was that, during the two weeks I hadn't said anything, I had been continuously looking at a particular noticeboard. I felt sure that was where I was going to see the information I needed. As it turned out, a day after I had been told about the woman in Croatia, her daughter, who was staying in Findhorn, put up a poster on the same noticeboard. For the next few days, I tried to arrange a meeting with her to discuss it, but nothing seemed to fit. The following morning, I woke particularly early and felt the urge to go to the early morning meditation, and, lo and behold, there, meditating right next to me when I opened my eyes, was the woman I was trying to meet up with.

During my time at Findhorn, I learnt the beauty of communing with nature and with the Divine. I had conversations about subjects that had never been in my awareness before. I reconnected with my healing and psychic energies and began using them as part of my everyday life. I enjoyed the diversities of spiritual practices, learnt to embrace prayer and to release expectations and outcomes. I knew how to work from a place of love and how to celebrate the joys of being alive, wherever I was, doing whatever I was doing right now. I was also able to thank William Bloom in person for being part of the journey that took me there. I heard just before I was about to leave that he would be visiting the Foundation for an event. It was to take place in the Park and I wasn't sure I would see him. However, the Universe had other plans and as I was coming out of a bathroom, wrapped in a towel, who should I bump into in the corridor outside my room but William? Thanking him wrapped in a towel wasn't what I'd been hoping for, but I knew that I had to take this opportunity. So I spoke his name and explained how grateful I was for the part he played. A few days later, it was time for me to leave, knowing that all was very, very well.

After all, I would be going back again. That I knew for sure.

Malinska, Krk, Croatia

So here I was, off again to a foreign country to stay with people I'd only spent a couple of hours with. For the first time in my life, I was travelling with a one-way ticket. I'd managed to get a flight for £15 to Trieste and I was going to bus it down to Rijeka. There I was to meet a member of the family I would be staying with and then get another bus to the island of Krk. As luck would have it, some members of the family were flying out that day to visit Findhorn, so I got a lift back with the person who had driven them up to Trieste.

When I arrived in the town of Rijeka, you can imagine my horror when the person from the family who had arranged the exchange with me handed me the keys to her very old gas-run car, expecting me to drive us over to the island of Krk. Apparently she wasn't a confident driver. *She* wasn't confident! Apart from its being a left-hand drive, held together with bits of tape and string, I had to climb in over the passenger seat as the driver's door wouldn't open. Now it was dark. She had insisted that I be rested and fed before we completed our journey. I was grateful for her thoughtfulness, but had I known that I would have been driving, I think I would have been happier to forego the food and rest. However, one of the things I'd learnt was what will be will be. I did mention that I wasn't insured to drive her car and I was concerned about all the legal stuff, especially being in a foreign country. My new-found friend waved her hand and said there was no problem, and, as it seemed the only way we would get to Krk, off we set. It must have been the slowest drive of my life. I was very grateful for the help of the angels that night. It was only near the end of my stay that I discovered that Croatian driving insurance is different from ours in that it is the car that is insured, not the driver. On that basis, I wouldn't have had anything to worry about.

Going to Croatia was an interesting experience. It was a combination of community and retreat. Sounds a paradox, I know, but in a part of the country where hardly any English was spoken I noticed that I didn't get dragged into other people's lives and dramas as I might have been if I overheard English-speaking conversations. Strangely, towards the end of my three-month stay, I was unknowingly tuning into the language, and if I was lying on the beach I seemed to know what was being said. What I hadn't expected after arriving back in the UK was to find myself dreaming in Croatian. Odd, as I didn't consciously know how to speak more than a few common phrases in the language.

What I felt I needed when leaving Findhorn was to go somewhere where I could connect with my femininity and with nakedness on all levels. I had grown up as a tomboy, mainly, I suppose, because, apart from one girl I played with, all of the children were boys. So it was a case of, 'if I didn't play with them,

I'd be on my own'. I was therefore involved in all their rough and tumble games and, of course, playing football, trolley building and tree climbing. When I was about fourteen and had given up my seat on a bus to an elderly man, he smiled back and said 'thank you, sonny'. It really hit me then that I was a girl and I felt a bit confused. I grew up with two younger brothers and it seemed to me that being a boy was the best deal. I guess they may not have seen it that way. Later on in life, when I was having children, I knew that I would only have boys. After all, I wouldn't know what to do with a girl, would I? I felt I had little experience of being a girl myself, and even less, as time went on, of being a woman. This was going to be an opportunity to set aside time to reconnect with the feminine part of me. To become comfortable with my own body and to know how that might feel.

I also wanted to strip bare the external layers and to connect with my core. Over the years I had developed many protective layers and I was beginning to feel that they no longer served me. Some had already fallen away, both in Skyros and at Ruskin. I wanted to let them all go one by one and see what was beneath. I think some people at Findhorn wondered why I needed to go away to do this. I agree that I could do it anywhere. But Findhorn is a working community, and I wanted to do this and wanted to do it now. I felt I needed to find a retreat, and Croatia, with its wonderful temperatures, seemed perfect. I wanted to feel the sun on my body and release the layers of winter clothes. I would be stripping physically, as well as on all the other levels. It was also something I felt I needed to do on my own, and how better to do that than in a foreign country?

Although the house and island I went to drew tourists during the months of July and August, they were mainly Croatian, Italian, German and Slovenian. So, as I said previously, I heard very little English spoken. In fact, I only heard about a dozen English-speaking voices during the three months I was there, and of those there were a group of four Australians, an American and a Canadian. Obviously, if I spoke English, the majority of the locals and indeed the tourists would speak it back to me. I had the best of both worlds: anonymity or company, whichever was my need. I didn't have to travel far to find some quiet space. I had a choice. There was either a short walk along the coast or the roof terrace of the family home where I lived.

The exchange I had agreed to in Scotland also included my commitment to assist from time to time in the family business. On the days on which visitors moved in and out of the house, I would help with the cleaning and preparation of the rooms. It felt a bit like Findhorn on a Saturday morning. I would also do some administrative tasks and assist the owners in setting up an English version of their website to enable them to sell their house. It was family-owned and there were three generations who lived there, four when one of the daughters came home with her boys. When one of their summer helpers left during the season, I volunteered to water the vegetable, fruit and flower gardens each evening. This was a real joy. It was very meditative and would take about ninety minutes in all. As I was only able to do it when the sun had gone down, it was a lovely way to end the day. All the work was a pleasure, and it also allowed me the free time I needed to do the work I wanted to do for myself.

Again, I had the best of both worlds with regards to living with the family. It was a custom there that if you worked together you ate together. As a vegan, it took a while to explain my dietary requirements, and I'm sure there might have been a few hurt feelings to start with regarding the meat, wheat, dairy, etc. However, as time went by they got used to it and ceased to offer me the things I couldn't eat. The grandparents could not speak English, although Grandmother understood a fair amount and did have a few words. The daughter with whom I had made the arrangement spoke English very well, as did her daughters. The two grandchildren were very fluent as well. All except the grandparents had paid a visit to Findhorn at some time in their lives. Things must have worked out quite well for the family, because when August came around and the women with the exception of the grandmother wanted to go off for four days to a sun-moon dance in Slovenia, I was asked to manage the business. It was explained that Grandmother would help me. I was happy to do it and didn't even give the language issue much of a thought. As it turned out, there weren't any language issues. The guests, Grandmother and I found a way to communicate with each other and meet each other's needs. It was a wonderful communication experience and I realised that it seemed easier to get along, perhaps, even more than with those who speak the same language. I don't know about you, but often I have spoken to someone who speaks the same language as me and we have had misunderstandings where words mean different things to each of us. Also, there is often a lack of checking in with each other to ensure that we are being understood. In some way or another, we seemed to do that naturally with all the languages going on. The intention, of course, was to understand and be understood, which I think sometimes in our everyday conversations gets forgotten.

I was very happy to do some family contract work while I was there. There were often issues arising between members of the family, especially with balancing the work and family life. We also did some work around roles and responsibilities, wants and needs. I can remember that things got very heated on one occasion. It was near the end of the season and, just a couple of days before eighteen guests were due to arrive to do a workshop centred on the house and family, one member of the family said she was leaving. We held a forum: something I'd learnt at the Foundation, which I think was introduced to them by a German community called Zeg. I have used it many times. Basically, a forum is opened by clapping, which clears the space. People are invited to air what is alive for them at that particular time; they are asked to speak from a place of I and not to look directly at anyone they may be referring to. Once the person is finished and seated again, everyone claps regardless of whether they agree with what has been said or not. Through this process, we eventually found a place where the family were able to meet and from there we put together a contract. It worked very well and the workshop was a great success, as was our working together on it. Based on its success, when another family issue arose which affected all four generations I was asked to work with them again. I was very grateful to be asked to assist in that way, especially as I had felt so well cared for during my stay there. I've always been very keen on mediation work. I suppose that may be why I have been drawn to the union work I got involved with and the voluntary work.

By the end of the three months, I felt like one of the family.

Even Grandfather let me do the watering without feeling the need to watch over me towards the end. I didn't mind because I knew the garden was so important to him. The food grown went a long way to feeding them, so I realised its importance, and also it had always been his responsibility. However, he had become a bit wobbly on his legs and often needed to rest. So I'd take a chair out for him and he would sit and chatter away to me in Croatian, letting me know what he wanted me to do. As time went by, there were fewer and fewer instructions and eventually I was allowed to go solo, but I was always expected to check in with him before and afterwards. It was a pleasure to do so; I had grown fond of him, as I had the rest of the family.

The area of inner processing I was working on was accomplished also. One by one, the layers were looked at, examined and released. I found the women on the island were at ease and, it appeared to me, quite provocative with their femininity, so it seemed that I was in the right place. I had a lot of time to think, journal and process, and in between I was able to soak up the sun that always seems to feed me. I notice how my body yearns for it at times. I was able to swim in warm, crystal-clear waters, skinny-dip under the full moon and dance naked on the roof terrace. I was happy with what I'd been able to do in such a short space of time. I'd become acquainted with my body wisdom, my femininity, my intuition, and had removed quite a few of the layers that no longer served me. After my return, I discovered that I had also been working on 'being in the now'. It was only when I was sharing with a friend of mine and he described some of the revelations of a book by Eckhart Tolle he was reading that it clicked with me. It was strange because, before I had left Findhorn, Eckhart had visited the Foundation to do a workshop. Although everyone was trying to get time off to go to at least one of his sessions, I hadn't felt the call. For some reason, I felt that if I was around it, I would capture what I needed anyway. I had no idea why I felt that, as it wasn't something I'd thought of before, but it seemed to make sense to me. In fact, the nearest I got to Eckhart the whole time he was there was to serve him dinner one evening when he was visiting Cluny. When I read his book at the invitation of my friend, I realised that I had been working in line with his book. Something else quite interesting happened regarding his book, *The Power of Now*. When I picked it up from the library, I opened it about a quarter of the way in and started reading. I wasn't able to put it down, so I decided to carry on reading from that point and thought I'd catch up on the beginning once I'd got to the end. The strange thing was that when I went back to the beginning I just couldn't engage with it. After four or five pages I gave it up as a bad job. I wondered what might have happened if I had started at the beginning of the book? My guess is that I wouldn't have read any of it.

Eckhart's book has cropped up with some of my clients, too. When I was giving a reading to one, I was drawn to discuss it with her as something she might be interested in. She looked at me in wonderment. Unwrapping the plastic bag she had with her, she produced a copy of his book. With another client, I raised his work and she told me a friend had bought her his calendar for Christmas, and it's cropped up on a few other occasions too.

As the days, weeks and months flew past I was feeling quite at home in Croatia. I think the family really enjoyed my being there, too. Grandmother had even offered me a contract to stay in my room over the winter period if I wanted to settle there to write my book. There would be very little work required from me, as everyone works flat out for July and August and then it goes back to being just the locals. It was amazing to watch the buildup when I arrived in June and the exodus during September. The thing I liked, apart from having fewer people around, was seeing the locals having time to have a coffee or a meal at a restaurant instead of working all the hours. As I walked around, I imagined it might have been like that in France after the liberation. People were reclaiming their land and living in a way that served them.

I had entered the country on a holiday visa, so I was technically only allowed to stay ninety days. As the days started to count down, I wondered if I would be going home to the UK. I also wondered whether if I did go back it would be to stay or whether I'd hop on the next plane out. It felt as if I was open to all and all was possible. I decided that if I was meant to go back to the UK, I didn't want to travel on a bus all the way up to Trieste to get a cheap flight back home. So I put a request out to the Universe: if I was meant to go home, I wanted a reasonably cheap flight from the island or nearby. Currently, there was only one flight a week from the island to London, and the cost of that flight was £300, which was way over my budget. I got to know some of the locals very well, particularly the women in the agency where I used the Internet. It was about ten days before my time was up when one of them asked me if I was planning on going home or not. I explained I wasn't sure but if I was going I needed a cheap flight. A couple of days later, she had some information for me about a one-off flight that would be leaving the island on what would be my eighty-ninth day in the country. It was at a reasonable price, too. A couple of phone calls later and there was a ticket with my name on it.

On the day I left, there were two flights leaving one after another. I don't know why, but when the flight was called I got up with my ticket and got in line. It was a while before I realised that most of the people around me were speaking French and I had got into the queue for the flight to Paris. So off I trotted to sit down next to a couple of Australian women and we started chatting. By the time our flight was called about twenty minutes later, I had mislaid my ticket. I'm not meant to be going, I thought. I searched everywhere and couldn't find it. The queue was quite short by now, as most people had boarded the plane, so I approached the flight attendant, explaining my predicament in the hope that I would be allowed a few more minutes to search for my ticket.

'No,' was her reply.

I had visions of the plane going off without me when she continued. 'No problem. I remember you checking in. Please take a seat on board.' I guessed I was meant to be leaving Croatia, because following on from 9/11 I hadn't expected to board any plane without a ticket. The UK it was to be, then.

Reading, Berkshire, England

When I got back to Reading, which had been my starting point a few years earlier, I was wondering where my journey would take me next. I'd been in touch with a friend who was looking after a case of winter clothes for me while I was in Croatia. She had said that I could stay at her home for a few nights while I decided what I wanted to do. She was living with her boyfriend at his place, so I would have the house to myself. A couple of nights later, she asked me if I'd be interested in redecorating her house top to bottom, as she wanted to sell it. In exchange, I could live there rent free. I heard myself say, 'Yes.'

'Heard myself' was right. It even puzzled me. I remember thinking, I don't decorate; I move. Also, I'd had very little experience. One of the things that came to mind was something that had been said to me when I was working in the maintenance department in Findhorn. 'It isn't always necessary to have experience to do a job; just tune into it like anything else and see what needs to be done and how best to do it.' OK, I thought, let me give it a go. I also wanted to carry on my 'studying'. Now I was in the third year of my 'degree' – first year Ruskin, second Findhorn. This year was going to be up to me to shape. So how would that look?

I joined a psychic development group, got attuned to Reiki. I also started to wonder where all these people who were living in Reading had been when I lived here before. It was a great eighteen months, and I met some interesting people and was offered a few jobs that helped me keep the wolves at bay and a roof over my head. It seemed quite synchronistic that, when I'd finished decorating my friend's house, I was offered a job by another acquaintance who had property. She was willing to let me have one of her studio flats in central Reading in exchange for computerising and organising her office for her.

The flat only had the essentials – hob, fridge, washing machine and bed – so I put an advert in the energy magazine that my psychic development tutor ran and, lo and behold, I ended up with a furnished flat. I had said that I only wanted things that people were hoping to get rid of because I didn't want to add to consumerism. Can you imagine the impact of my going out and buying everything I needed when everything I needed appeared to be in the back of someone's cupboard? It also appeared they were only too happy for me to help them clear clutter. I explained that I could only accept things that I needed, so I turned down about five televisions, a few computers, although I was grateful to be given a laptop, and many other duplicates. In fact, during the year I lived there I was given three laptops. The first was stolen; I was burgled when I was away one weekend. The second crashed and the third is the one that I'm currently using. Everything, it seemed, was colour coordinated, too. My flat had a blue theme going on. That's a healing colour for me. There definitely was some healing going on, too. For all of my life it has always been very easy for me to give. Very difficult, I realised, to receive. It was very strange. I'd offered to do things in exchange for the gifts I received. Some people had a Reiki session or a reading; someone even asked for some home-made soup when I was thrilled that they were going to give me a food processor and told them that I loved making soups. People's generosity is quite amazing. It wasn't something I had ever thought of doing before, but it seemed to work out well for everyone. I'm sure we could do more along those lines, don't you think? I know some social enterprises have been set up to help those who are socially and financially disadvantaged. I believe there is even a designer Oxfam shop in Knightsbridge, so who knows?

The intention behind my staying in Reading was writing this book. I decided that, no matter how lovely Croatia was in the summer, the house would be very cold in the winter, as it didn't have any central heating. The blend of cold, me and writing was not going to work. I therefore had turned down the offer. However, I got distracted and, as I became caught up in earning money, time for the book got less and less. I did very much enjoy the jobs I had, though. For a few months I was driving children with special needs to and from school, and after that I had a job with Mencap, where I was supporting adults who were living in their own homes to make life choices. I remember walking down to the beach one day in Croatia and a thought about unconditional love coming into my mind. I wondered if I would be able to love people with special needs. I had no idea where it came from or why I was thinking about it at the time. I wondered now if I was being prepared for the work I would engage in when I got back. Or if I was being shown that I was learning to love unconditionally. Whatever – it seemed an answer to a prayer. I'd begun to realise that this communication between me and Source was definitely working. Especially if I released expectations of outcome.

Living in Reading was the first time in my life I had lived on my own. I hadn't realised that before. I noticed I was having this urge to reach out to the community around me. I was contemplating how I could do this when I thought of giving a talk. What would be the subject matter? I felt I had lots I could talk about, but no one thing seemed to surface above anything else. I was having dinner with a friend one evening and mentioned this wish to her.

'So what would you talk about?' she said.

It was as if I were hearing this question for the first time. That's when the word 'prayer' came in and I remember cringing at the thought.

'Why prayer and why me?' I asked myself.

But I knew this pattern fairly well by now and when something chooses me rather than letting me choose it I tend to go with it. I was equally surprised by my friend's response when she said, 'Oh, great, I'd like to come along to that.'

Only a month later, another new idea presented itself. This was the birth of Inspirational Voices. This time, the Universe wasn't suggesting I do it as a lone project; instead, the idea was to collaborate with three of my dearest friends. How could I approach them, I wondered. I knew they were already up to their eyes with their own work and families. Surely the Universe had got this wrong? So, as instructed, I emailed and waited for the refusals to come back. One after one the replies came in and they were all very excited and wanted to be involved. It's currently a work in progress and we are pleased to be taking baby steps towards our dream. It's great to be working together on a project that meets our need for both individuality and community. What we are enjoying most is how our collaborative work is not like any other work experience we have previously been part of, except of course for my recent lone inner experiences.

I began to notice how much I'd changed. I guess that maybe some people would not have noticed it as I had. Maybe because, while in the past I may have done some of the things I was doing now, I would have been doing them under someone else's umbrella. It might have been my place of work, my social environment or a relationship. I'd always been a great number two, a good support person. Let the person who had the dream tell me what it was and I would help them achieve it by playing my part. Now it seemed it was my turn to be a leader of dreams, in particular mine. Hopefully, by doing so, I can inspire others to live theirs. I suppose the subtle difference, which perhaps only I know, is how I feel about doing what I do best. I now feel more confident about it, especially as I'm putting forward something I can talk about from the heart, something that I am passionate about rather than someone else's passion.

My passion now was writing my book, and I felt as if I had to give everything up to give it my full attention. After all, this vision had come to me about four years previously when a thought came into my head to do something different from managing IT contracts. I'd arranged some quiet time so that I could visualise what my future might look like. When I did this, I noticed myself going down a corridor with many doors, one of which drew me. As I went through the door, I could see myself in what looked like a lecture room, speaking to many people. I watched this for a while, noticing how comfortable I felt with what was being shown to me. It was as if I were watching a film, and as the 'camera' scanned down my arm it showed that my hand was resting on a book. I picked it up and held it and referred to it. It was my book, one that I had written. That belief has stayed with me over the last few years when I've been on my journey of reawkening, and now is the time I've decided to stop carrying it around with me. It's time to bring the dream to a reality and write it and see it published. It's amazing how light my back feels now that I no longer have to carry it around. For me it's an example of many things I have chosen to carry around with me over the years instead of dealing with them at the time. How could I make this dream a reality? I had worked out by now that I needed to release one thing in order to make space for the new to come in. So the job with my accommodation had to go and I needed to give notice, regardless of having nowhere currently presenting itself for me to live. The process that followed is worthy of a chapter in its own right, but in short I chose to be present with myself at every moment. I'd learnt the power of being in the now and being a witness to my own journey. I honoured each feeling as it arose and remembered Source's advice in allowing time to play. Two poems came to me after a visualisation I had at one of my psychic development group sessions. I was shown the story of my book run backwards. First I was shown myself speaking with Michael Parkinson on his chat show and then there I was signing books and talking to people in Waterstone's. I was then shown it being printed, and as the pages were flying by on the presses I noticed sparkles in the air. As I watched the process, I felt I was getting the message that a certain energy needed to be carried through all stages of this book so that the reader would get the sparkles too. After the visualisation session, we were encouraged to write down a message and the following poems flowed through me.

Golden Eyes

Golden eyes are the sweetest thing,
They open up your heart strings.
You flow and glow, and the words come out.
You do not have to think what they're about.
They come from you, and you and you.
There are the sun and then the moon.
They come and go and flow and flow.
You don't need to think because you know.
Life is just a game, you see.
A game where you become me.
Yes, it's me, the God you know,
It's me, it's you and together we grow.
Just remember to be and not to do,
And all life's challenges will drop from you.
To be is such a lovely state,
You are what you are – it is your fate.
I love you as you are today.
I love you now you've learnt to play.
So listen now and don't forget:
Life isn't for worrying, it's just to beget.

From you grows life, and so it goes.
I want you dancing, now up on those toes!
For when you're carefree you work best for me,
It is your time to wander and be free.
I need you rested and sitting in state,
I need you loving with an open gate.
There's no need to polish or drive your van.
There's no need to think you need a man.
You are the man, you are everything.
When I watch you grow my heart just sings.

All is Light

All is light – all is well.
Let what you need come to you.
Trust that it will.
Take time out to be.
Find the place by the sea.
Feel the sun upon your face.
Feel your spirit fill with grace.
Watch the children giggle and play.
Watch the sunbeams at the end of the day.
Feel the air as it caresses your face.
Be the star you watch in space.
Be the sand beneath your feet.
Be the people you will meet.
Love them all as you do today.
But never forget there's always time to play.

Ashbury, England

As I write this book, Icknield Rise in Ashbury is the current 'community' I am part of. I feel so at home here and play with the idea that it might be my home for a while. I've two weeks left within my three-month deadline for writing my book and I feel confident in completing this first draft. A friend from Ruskin is planning to proofread it for me. Another is exploring with me some illustration work about the book and some cards I'd like to do to accompany it. Nick Williams, a published author, kindly offered to read a few chapters and give me some feedback – bless you, Nick – and I am putting a book proposal together. I must be on the right track because I'm receiving everything I need to put this together. It has been very important for me to keep to my initial deadline of three months because at first it felt as if I wanted Source to trust me; that my word was my bond. After all, if you are going to collaborate with someone then there needs to be trust. Of course I realised straight away that Source has always trusted me. It was I who wanted to trust myself. To be self-disciplined enough to work on this project. I've witnessed nothing but love for me over the last few years. I don't doubt for one minute that it has always been there. I just had my defence shield up and it wasn't able to get through. When things go smoothly for me, I trust I'm on the right track, even though I may not know the big picture. Sometimes I'm just shown one step at a time. If it flows, I go with it. If I hit a brick wall, then I've taken the wrong turn or the time is not right.

I also love being 'at home' here. This is the place I love living and working in. So another prayer has been answered for me. I enjoy making homemade bread and soups and working in the garden and on our organic allotment. Living with others is wonderful, too. We are only three as I write now and the house is for five, so I am interested in how and when that will play out. There are, of course, the two owners who are part of our group but live in another house in the village. I've also enjoyed getting to know the people who live in the village and experiencing the joys of this part of the country. I've started to run workshops and groups for psychic development, spiritual dreambuilding and Reiki. Working with other people who want to heal and build their dreams from a spiritual base is an absolutely joy for me.

I feel I now have completed my degree in Spiritual Dreambuilding and this book is the equivalent of my Master's. It has truly been a gift to myself. I'm so glad I trusted that I was worth it. I continually thank Source, the angels, fairies and my guides for the support and guidance they have given me. On a physical level, I'm grateful to all the people and organisations who have helped me awaken my true self and are continually aiding me in building my dreams and the dreams of others. I have been able to bring joy and laughter through the release of tears and I am willing to help bring people home.

Obviously there was more to come from my living in Ashbury other than writing my book, and in the living will come the telling.

***** Exercises *****

Community – what does this word mean for you? What are its values? Why not write down a few sentences describing its essence? List the communities you are currently part of. Are they congruent to your values? Is there anything you can do to transform that? What gifts and talents do you offer your communities? What do you receive from them?

Synchronicity – how have you noticed this playing out in your life? Have books, ideas, opportunities, people come your way at just the right time? If it has been unnoticed so far, why not invite it to play out for you over the next couple of weeks? Keep a journal and record events daily, as sometimes you only notice these synchronicities retrospectively.

Who or what has inspired you? What have been your most inspirational moments? Was it a person, a place or an event that inspired you? What aspect touched you? How does it make you feel? How do or can you express this in your life? Does it inspire you to shape some changes?

Creativity – often our creativity can be suppressed and we get blocked. Why not allow yourself to reconnect with it in whatever form it wants to take? It could be body movement, sound or working with materials. Try not to put a box around what creativity is or how it can be expressed. Tune into your inner self and see how it wants to play out. Try to give yourself a chunk of time each week to work with this. Maybe do it with friends or family members. Do not judge or make comments on anyone's expressions; just appreciate and be grateful for the connection. See if it has a message for you.

Sharing Groups/Circles – have you every shared in this way before? Would you like to experience being part of a group where you could share on a regular basis with like-hearted people? Maybe you could join or start one for parents, women, men, spiritual sharing, healing, meditation, prayer, Reiki, psychic development, etc?

Co-listening – why not try this out with a friend, partner or member of your family (particularly with your children – whatever age)? Spend some time telling the other person what's alive in you right now and how you feel. Know that this time will be uninterrupted. The person listening will not be reflecting back to you either verbally or non-verbally, their judgements only the words you have spoken. Notice how you feel when you hear what you have said. Notice how you feel when holding the space for someone else to be heard.

Noticing Resistance – often we get many ideas coming our way. Notice how you feel when they first arrive – you may feel enthused or excited by an idea's potential. Very quickly that might be followed by resistance which may manifest as distractions – physical, emotional or mental; self-doubt, ridicule – internal or external; needing to tidy the house, getting something to eat, being too busy, feeling unwell. Notice these reactions and what takes you away from your true self, the part of you that wants to nurture and grow the ideas that have come to you as gifts. If you recognise any of these distractions, well done – you have just met your 'ego', and it's your ego's job to prevent you from fulfilling your dreams. Don't let it. Reframe your relationship with it and watch the transformation.

Work – whether paid or voluntary, either in the home or externally, can you describe what you are doing right now as 'work as love in action'? Are you able to feel that when you carry out all the tasks in which you are involved, you are able to do so from a place of love? Try starting each new task with a loving thought for a day; if your task takes a long period of time, set a timer for every thirty minutes and check in to see if you are still coming from a place of love. What do you notice from this way of working? What is reflected back to you? If you have a pattern or a preferred practice, why not play with it and see how you feel doing it in a different way, at a different speed, at a different time of day, in a different room?

Who or what niggles you, presses your buttons, irritates you? Make a list of the things that have attracted your attention in this way over the last week or month. Reflect now on each of them and see if there is something in you which is seeking healing. Try not to blame or judge outwardly or inwardly; merely witness what it is and enquire of it what attention it needs and how it may be healed. Identify the qualities, strengths and weaknesses and separate them from the behaviour.

Prayer – if it isn't part of your life at the moment, I'd encourage you to try to create a few prayers of your own and see how powerful they are. I'd encourage you also to allow some time for silence at the end of your prayer so that Source can respond to you.

Living in Gratitude – give yourself a little time at the end of each day and list ten things that you have been blessed with. Try this for a week without repeating things and notice the changes in your life.

Are there aspects of yourself from which you feel disconnected? Could it be your sexuality, gender, age, emotions, feelings, body, mind, spirituality? Allow time for the response and, when something surfaces, allow further time for what is beneath the surface, too. Explore in whatever way feels comfortable to you (visualisation, meditation, movement, prayer) what may have caused this disconnection. Take time to be with it, hold it and love it and ask it what it needs to feel part of the whole again.

What would your 'degree' look like? What would it be called? What would you include? Is it already available or do you need to build it? Who or what can help you build this dream?

Mystery Tour

Life before Reawkening

WHEN I STARTED THIS JOURNEY FIVE YEARS AGO, I COULD never have imagined where it would take me or the stops I would make along the way. In truth, it really was and still is a mystery tour. I definitely would have scoffed at the idea of being a spiritual teacher, writing a book and travelling around the world working with individuals and groups, helping them to connect with their Source, their purpose and their dreams. I would never have imagined that I would take the opportunities to study in Oxford, live in a community for a year, live and work in Croatia, travel to America or become at times a nomad.

Having been brought up as a Roman Catholic, I rebelled aged eleven when I wasn't given what I deemed to be satisfactory answers to the questions I was asking. For me, there was no walking the talk. As a young child, what I saw were people going to church, dressed up in their Sunday best, smiling at everyone, reciting the service in Latin (most of which they didn't understand – well, I didn't, anyway) – it infuriated me. They would nod their heads at the sermon and then shake the priest's hand at the end of the service. I wanted to stand up and screech, 'There is something wrong with this.'

I was angry at being told how 'bad' I was – that I was full of sin. I knew I wasn't bad. I felt I was a beautiful, innocent child. However, the more they told me the more I wondered. Yet I saw what I interpreted as a lot of 'bad' around me. Especially from some of the people in the church, some of whom I was at the mercy of on a daily basis at the Roman Catholic school I attended. Don't get me wrong; this is not a dig at the Roman Catholic Church, or indeed any religion. It is merely something I witnessed and interpreted as a child and it was my truth at the time.

I remember wondering why there was so much fear around. Why was I so scared of the nuns, priests and canon? I only remember one priest who I wasn't afraid of. I wish I could remember his name, but he was younger than the rest and had soft ginger hair and smiled a lot. It felt as if what he said made sense to me because it was more about being loved than about fear. I suppose at the time that was what I was searching for – an opportunity to be loved. It wasn't something I was experiencing a lot in my young life. Again, I'm not putting blame out onto teachers and family, but it was what I was experiencing on that part of my journey.

So, like a good girl, I would go to church on Sundays and take my two little brothers with me. Well, most Sundays, and then when I didn't go I would hardly sleep at night, knowing that when I was at school the following morning I would be asked if I had attended Mass. I was so scared to say 'no', for fear of the punishment that would follow. For me, the worst bit would be the verbal chastisement and humiliation. When I couldn't face that any more, I would lie. So when it came time to go to confession I would then have two things instead of one to confess. That's what didn't make sense to me. Surely I wasn't the only child confessing to being afraid to tell the truth.

I also thought there must have been more to forgiveness than saying three Hail Marys and an Act of Contrition; at least, I hoped so, otherwise people could do anything bad and it would be OK. It seemed that I was being asked to recite it like a nursery rhyme, and that was not enough for me. I see now that I was looking for something a little more meaningful and deeper. I also believe there was something deeper in what was being offered, but I didn't feel it at the time.

What can be right about forcing a five-year-old to drink milk? When I told my teachers that I didn't drink milk they wouldn't listen. So I was stood over and told to drink it up through a straw. My idea then was to sip some up into my mouth and then, when they weren't looking, to spit it out. They must have met children like me before because they wouldn't take their eyes off me and then told me to swallow. I couldn't do it, so shook my head. The next thing I knew was that my nose was being held so that I would have to swallow. Guess they hadn't thought about the other option, the one I went for, which was to spit it out. It wasn't my intention for it to go all over them, but that's what happened and obviously they decided I needed to be punished for that. It was a time when corporal punishment was used in schools and we would be lined up after lunch to recite why we were there and then told how many strikes across the hands we were going to receive.

With regards to milk, it was only in my fifties, when I had started listening to my body, that I decided to cut out all dairy products. I was going through the menopause at the time and it was suggested that it might be a natural way to help the symptoms I was experiencing. Can you believe it? Not only did it aid that process, but I have never since experienced any of the bronchial ailments that had previously plagued my life from childhood. I remember saying that my chest was always my weakest point. If there was anything going, then I would get it. I've had bronchitis, pleurisy, pneumonia and more chesty coughs than you can imagine. However, I've not experienced any of these since I released dairy from my diet. I wonder now if that five-year-old Jacqueline really was wise enough to know that dairy products were not what her body needed and then got it knocked out of her. After all, who is going to listen to a five-year-old and believe she knows better than the adults around her? I have this belief that as children we are born wise. We have all the inner knowledge that we need, and by the time we are five or seven it goes to sleep or, in some cases, is knocked out of us.

My heart goes out to the children in the world today who are being labelled and who are not being listened to and supported, in particular those known as the Indigo and Crystal children. There have been many books written about these children and there are numerous websites you can visit to get more information, especially if you think you or a child around you is one. Some adults alive on the planet now were born as early Indigo and Crystal children so that they could help the vast numbers of children coming through at this time. We are teaching and labelling children and teenagers as difficult when we are not offering them what they really need. Our ways of teaching and parenting are out of line with their needs. If society were a business, we would be researching what our clients wanted and finding a way to see how best we could serve them. Then we would have a thriving business. Is it just too simple?

I remember once being struck several times with a ruler because of what happened during a lunch hour. Again, it seemed so unfair to me. The school wasn't large enough to have its own dining hall and we would walk, crocodile-like, up to a nearby community centre to receive meals that had been ferried there from some far-off place. Something, I can't remember what, had happened while we were waiting to collect our dinners. We were therefore put on 'silent dinner', which meant no speaking. There I was, eating my dinner, when the boy next to me fainted head first into my rice pudding. I let out such a yelp that one of the people 'caring' for us yanked me by my arm and dragged me from the bench I was sitting on. She was completely ignoring my friend, who was by then lifting up his food-covered face from my pudding plate. As I was being dragged to a corner, I tried to explain what had happened but was continually told to be silent. Eventually some other children spoke up and someone went to look after him. Can you believe I was still punished because they thought I could have responded more quietly? Thinking back, maybe I had been labelled a 'difficult child' and therefore the first thought was that I was doing something wrong, maybe trying to get attention. Who knows? What if I were? Why would wanting attention be such a bad thing?

There were other events, but honestly I no longer have a need to remember them. It was when I was being told at the age of eleven that my senior school was going to be the convent that I begged my parents not to send me there. I had received the harshest of treatments from the nuns in my school, so there was no way I was going to go to a school that was full of them. As the person I am now, I don't label all nuns and priests as bullies, but as a child I believed they were all the same. That had been my experience. It was the first time in my life that I felt I had been heard. I don't remember the process or why I was allowed to influence the decision. Maybe I didn't? Maybe it suited my parents; I don't know. What I do remember is that I was over the moon that I didn't have to go there.

During my life, I have often been drawn back to churches and, in later years, to other places of worship or ritual. When my children were born, I wanted to allow them to make their own decisions about religion. I remember once, when I was taking them for a walk in Plymouth, we passed a church and I asked them if they would like to go in. They were keen, but as we got to the door I noticed it was locked. There was a sign that said 'for entry, please go to vicarage'. So off we trotted, only to be looked at quizzically by a vicar who said, 'You just want to look around?'

'Yes, please. I thought it would be nice for my children to come inside while it's quiet.'

'Perhaps it would be best if you came when it was open for a service.'

'It would be great if you could let us look now,' I said.

He then went on to tell me the opening times. I wasn't expecting him to drop everything to let the children be inside, but I did feel his reluctance to offer any time other than a service.

Interesting, I remember thinking, before taking the boys off for a game of football in the park. Although I do remember taking them to Sunday school on a few occasions, I don't think they have been back since, except for the usual weddings and funerals. Mostly the same could be said for me.

I've also had the opportunity to do a fair bit of travelling in my life, mostly on holidays. I began to notice that often I would stumble across a church or temple – something was pulling me and has never let go. I always felt that there was something behind the people who fronted these places with which I needed to connect.

When I was nearing fifty, I made a decision to live my life fully from that moment on. I thought I could capture some of the things that I would have liked to have done when I was younger, such as take a gap year, travel, go to university and work for myself. It was then that I started to connect with my spirituality. It didn't have that label to describe it then, but, looking back, that's what I would call it – my spiritual reawkening.

I had done some of the usual things and some not so usual in the years leading up to that time. I'd had two broken marriages and one ten-year relationship that had also come to an end. I'd had an estranged relationship with my mother for most of my life. I'd had various jobs but not the one I had really wanted. That one had eluded me. I wanted to be at home with my children. I had wanted to be a stay-at-home mum. Becoming a single mum and the financial constraints that came with that helped persuade me to find a job and not be a 'drain on society's resources', as I think it was put at the time. I was also looking for something. I didn't know what it was, but I knew it was something that made me feel alive. Something was missing in my life and I couldn't put my finger on it. I thought it might be a career or maybe a boyfriend. Something that would enable me to feel better than I was feeling. What I attracted, it seemed, was drama and more drama. I had broken relationships, ill health and a big front I was showing to the world.

So at fifty the changes started with learning to love myself, followed by discovering the work I was born to do, then by connecting to what I called my dreams and turning them into a reality. I discovered that I had choices. I know I've always had them. In the past, however, I think I did things because I thought I didn't have any choice, rather than positively choosing to do something. I hope that's making sense to you. For example, when I left home aged seventeen I ran to my boyfriend's house for help. I wanted him to help me find a place of my own to live. What I got was, 'You can live here with me and my gran.'

I don't want to sound ungrateful, but it wasn't what I wanted. I needed space for me. I said, 'No, I want a place of my own. Can you help me find a flat?' His response was that if I didn't live with him then I would be 'dumped'. It was then that I felt I had no choice. I couldn't go back home – I'd escaped that – and I didn't want to be alone. Or, more importantly, I didn't think I could make it on my own. So I accepted the offer and moved in. I wasn't being true to myself; I was compromising, which is fatal. That doesn't mean that I can't find a balance, but to compromise with oneself or with another means you give things up rather than find something that works.

My having discovered the freedom of choice, the world was my oyster, so to speak. Life is worth living and is a far cry from the time in my life when I attempted suicide. So I chose to learn and was thirsty for knowledge; I wanted to try it all. Why not? I believe this was quite a difficult time for some of the people around me. I was giving up my home, my job, expanding my awareness, and I suppose in some ways I was challenging their belief systems. It wasn't my intention to do so, yet I've discovered along the way that this is what happens. Sometimes I feel like Rambo; if I take a step in a certain direction, a grenade seems to go off in someone's face. Although it's not deliberate, I know it's the role I must play to be true to myself and my purpose. Seeing the transformation does help a lot. Likewise, when I feel it happening to me, I know to look inside and see what is crying out for attention.

The next stop on my Mystery Tour was in a bookshop. I had picked up a book (actually, it threw itself off the shelf in Waterstone's and landed in my hand, but who is going to believe that?) by Diana Cooper called *A Little Light on Angels*. I hadn't had the chance to read more than a couple of chapters, but the piece that caught my imagination was when she wrote 'I believe we are constantly being protected by our guardian angels and other spiritual helpers. How else could we, with our limited mortal sense, race down motorways at immense speed and miss each other?' I couldn't stop laughing as I visualised angels sitting on the top of all the cars.

Reading that piece jerked me back a couple of years. I had been driving to a conference; a friend was looking after my children for the weekend. As it started on the Friday evening, I needed to travel on the M25 around 5 p.m., one of the busiest times. I was in the middle lane when my tyre burst and while trying to bring the car under control and to an appropriate halt I somehow managed to find myself sideways-on across the fast lane. It all happened in a microsecond; as I recall it now in slow motion, all I could see as I looked down the motorway was a mass of cars ploughing down in all three lanes. There was no way there wasn't going to be a collision and no way I wasn't for it. I remember noticing how odd it was that I didn't feel frightened. I'd done everything I could do and now I felt as if I were in someone else's hands. I closed my eyes, and when I opened them again there was a police officer talking to me from the passenger side. I looked down the motorway and all three lanes were stopped. The car that had been travelling behind me had stopped so close to my door that it was not possible to open it more than a couple of inches. There was another police officer talking to me from that side. Not one car on that busy motorway had crashed into another. I was so relieved. Firstly that I was alive, secondly that my children were not going to lose their mother and thirdly that I was travelling on my own. After the police officers had managed to take me to the hard shoulder and changed my tyre, I had to get back in and carry on with my journey. There was no one else to hand over the driving to.

After reading Diana's book and remembering that previous motorway encounter, I have a mantra that I use every time I start a journey: 'I ask the angels to guide and protect me and' (then I add the name of my car; when I owned one she was called Rosie and the one I borrowed was called Nubi) 'and all other people and property both in and around us. I ask that I and those around me drive with compassion, creating spaces and opportunities for all of us to get to where we need to be at a time that serves the highest good of all.'

I always love returning to Plymouth to see my friends and extended family living there. No wonder my elder son currently feels that he cannot leave the place. One day, I decided to go for a walk along a favourite beach. When I set off it was sunny and then a mist started to gather around me. My mood changed as well. I started to silently weep as I walked, remembering the deaths of my brother and sister-in-law and also the death of my marriage and what had followed. It was while this was happening that I remembered Diana's book. I remember looking upwards and saying that if there were such things as angels, something that would give me hope, particularly of life after death, then I'd like to have some proof, please. Two days later, when I had all but forgotten my request, I was lying in my bed, looking up at the ceiling. It was awash with angels. They were various shapes and sizes and of different shades of white and gold. There was a wonderful sound of music, too, and it appeared that I was up there with them, looking down on my body, which was still lying in my bed. Then, as quickly as it came, it was gone. It was as real as me sitting here writing this book. I've believed in angels ever since, even though at that time I wouldn't have thought of myself as a spiritual person. Since that time, I have sensed and seen them, but never quite in that way. I remember how accepting I was at the time that it was the truth. They did exist and they had shown themselves to me in all their glory.

The lesson that was to come my way following on from that experience was acceptance. That one didn't come so easily, though. I'm so grateful to the angels for their delightful way of bringing it to my attention. I was in a nomadic period. I had completed my course at Ruskin College and was due to start a three-month programme in the Findhorn Foundation in two months' time. As both of these offered live-in programmes, having previously given up my rented accommodation, I was faced with a summer of wandering. Fantastic, I remember thinking. When I was a child, I would often be teased by my father for walking around without any shoes on.

'If you carry on like that,' he said, 'you'll grow up to be a gypsy.'

Instead of instilling fear in me, it conjured up this wonderful vision of being a gypsy and wandering around the countryside in my painted wagon being pulled by a horse. Now it felt as if I had the opportunity to become one, albeit in my beautiful car called Rosie.

As it turned out, I wasn't to be homeless at all. I'm blessed with the number of friends I have, and I was accommodated by them throughout that period. The time I'm particularly referring to is when I was house-sitting for a friend in St Albans. She had gone to stay with her sister in Spain for three weeks and I had the place to myself. The weather was particularly warm and she had a beautiful secluded garden, which I took advantage of. I was doing a fair amount of journaling at the time and wanted to prepare myself for the months at Findhorn. At the time, I was working with my Diana Cooper Angel Cards, and it seemed that for every question I asked I received the 'Acceptance' card. In fact, I received it seven times in a row over that period. 'OK,' I said to the angels, 'I get the message.'

Getting it was one thing. Understanding it and grounding it

by living it was another. As my stay at my friend's house was ending, I didn't have anywhere planned to go next. The days ticked past and I wondered what I might do. So, on the penultimate day, I picked up the road atlas and opened a page.

'You must be joking,' I said as I saw the Wolverhampton/Birmingham area come up to greet me. Oh, well, I thought, I wonder which of these has my name on it. So I twirled the book around and then placed my finger on the page. When I opened my eyes, I noticed the pages were upside down, so I needed to turn it around to get a proper look. My finger had struck the edge of the page and I could see that I was on the edge of a town but needed to turn the page over to see what its name was. I couldn't believe my eyes when I saw it. It was York. I had always wanted to visit there but hadn't managed it thus far. This was about to change. At the same time, I remembered a woman I had met in Findhorn by chance along one of the corridors. We hadn't met before, but there was something about each other that we instantly recognised when we met. There was an instant rapport and intimacy. I gave her a call to ask if she was going to be free for catching up while I was visiting. I also wanted to check in with her about B&Bs in the area to see if she had any recommendations.

'No need for that. You can stay with me. Oh, and there's no need to worry about my cat. I've just had a word with him and everything will be OK.'

She had remembered that I was still a bit cautious around animals, especially cats. I'd been frightened of animals for most of my life, but since finding spirituality it seemed that my fear was changing of its own accord. What's more, I truly believed her when she said she had spoken to her cat about my fear and that everything would be OK. We actually became quite good friends during my stay. The cat and me, I mean. Since that time, I've been blessed to be able to communicate more widely: not just with the animal kingdom, but with trees, plants and the land.

So my journey, which had started off with an idea of liberation on a physical, emotional and mental level, opened out to embrace a spiritual perspective, too. At times I pray that it will continue that way, although on occasions a part of me does yearn to stop, to settle and make a base. I honour each of those parts and all the other parts of me that have now found a voice and someone who listens to them. There is no longer a need to seek attention. I have all the attention I need. All I need to do is ask myself for it and lovingly respond.

Life can be a mystery tour, and I suppose for each of us that might have a different feel to it. Some of us want to be sure of where we are going and what we can expect when we get there. Others want the adventure, the unexpected, and are open to whatever comes their way. There is no right or wrong, and there are many more possibilities than that I have alluded to. Sometimes, I think, it might be worth giving the mystery tour a go. After all, if I hadn't, who knows where I would be right now? If the bus sign had read 'Spirituality Tour – all aboard. Stopping at Oxford, Findhorn, Croatia and all places in between', I'm not sure I would have got on. What I do know now is that I wouldn't have missed this trip for anything.

***** Exercises *****

Have you ever taken a mystery tour? What was your experience? Would you be willing to experience another kind of mystery tour – a spiritual one? Why not try a virtual one?

The invitation is to organise some time in the near future when you can do this either alone or with a like-hearted friend. Maybe you'd like to talk each other through the steps, ensuring time for journeying and responses. So organise some uninterrupted time. Turn off your phones, put a 'do not disturb' sign on your door and either meditate or visualise what your mystery journey may look like.

What do you notice about your starting point? What mode of transport do you take? How many paths/roads are in front of you? What do they look like? What do the signposts say? What happens when you travel each path? Is the road straight/narrow/wide/wiggly? Does it have more paths off it? What do you see? Who do you meet? What does it feel like? What does the journey mean to you?

This journey can be taken in one sitting or in bite-size pieces over a period of time. Honour the journey by turning up when you said you would and find a way to capture the images/messages you get by journaling, drawing, recording – be as creative with the capturing as you feel appropriate. Afterwards, feel free to interpret what the symbols and messages are telling you. Notice any resistances you have in the recording that you didn't have in the visualisation.

If you like, why not play with some of the stopping-off points highlighted in this chapter in the same way? Take a trip with:

Childhood truths – is there anything you believed as a child that wasn't honoured by the adults/peer groups around you, which has become an adult truth for you? How would that experience help you feel differently towards the children/young people in your life now?

Places you've been drawn to – are there any places that keep pulling you back over the years? Places of worship, ancient sites, towns, rivers, countries? Explore why that is and what that means to you.

Connecting and fulfilling your dreams – are there things you have always wanted to do but think are impossible or keep putting off? Why don't you list them and give each one time to speak to you? What would it look/feel like to be living those dreams? Do you notice recurring thoughts about them or have either night/day dreams where they are played out? Are they asking for your attention? Look back at your list and see how it would feel to put a date next to them, one that you feel might be a realistic achievement date. What or who can support that dream? How do you feel now?

Choices – have there been times in your life when you felt you didn't have a choice? What if you were to revisit them now and see if there were any other options for you? Release any 'buts' from the scenario and just allow their voices to be heard. Sometimes it can be useful to stand back and look at a decision from another aspect.

Angels and the spirit world – have you had an experience in your life that you wondered how you survived or where you got the help you needed just at the right time? Who or what do you think may have influenced that? Do you know that angels and those in the spirit world are dedicated to helping us? All they need is for us to ask them. Try to remember to ask for help when you need it.

Words of wisdom – do you ever experience thoughts, ideas that have seemed alien to your current belief system, culture, and way of life, yet in some way seem to have a truth about them? Maybe you notice that there is a lack of initial acceptance? I think every thought is a spark from the Divine – what we choose to do with it is up to us. The invitation is to notice *your* thoughts and, more importantly, *your* reactions and responses to them.

Family and Relationships

Our Greatest Opportunities to Heal

IT SEEMS PECULIAR THAT THIS WAS THE PENULTIMATE chapter I was to complete before releasing this book for publication. So, being the sort of person I am, I was wondering why that was. When the original structure of the book came to me, I headed the chapter 'Family'. However, one morning I awoke and saw the heading change in my mind's eye to become the one you see above. It was then that I smiled.

Of course, I remember thinking, that's why it wasn't written before. Either I was leaving the best to last or I was resisting what potentially offered the greatest opportunity for me to heal.

Maybe it's a bit of both. As I'm editing this chapter, I'm gaining clarity around the answer, but, like many things that have happened since I agreed with Spirit to write this book, the insights have become clear to me when the time was right. And the circumstances have been put in place for them to play out. It appears that, even though I had confidence that there was enough material to commence writing this book, I'm now gaining even more insights from being part of this project. And that brings me joy.

It makes me laugh sometimes as I imagine God and his host of angels acting like project managers. I like to think that there is a project manager for everyone. Having been involved in many projects in the business world, I do know a fair amount about project management and the challenges that arise along the way. Including all the implications the smallest of changes can have. The ripple effect can be tremendous. So I imagine sometimes what it would be like to be a member of God's project team, receiving all these change management notes in the form of prayers, affirmations and intentions continually during the day.

All I can say is a big 'thank you' to the project manager in charge of my plan, as I know how constantly during my life I have changed my priorities. For instance: one minute I'll be concentrating on my writing, and to help that take place my project manager receives the information, contacts the relevant teams, identifies resources, explores potential hazards, looks at time constraints, financial implications, business partners etc. etc. Three hours later, I'm wondering if I ought to look at bringing in more money to sustain myself. So maybe I should be advertising my services by running workshops and groups? Or maybe the time is right for me to find a partner? So, of course, the project management team needs to build this in, and it's all change on the Jacqueline Iris Daly project again. How many times in my life have I done this? How many times in a month, a week or even a day sometimes? Not one word of moaning have I received from the management team. Not one. No criticism, no judgement, no blame, no reproach; only a 'how can we make this happen?' response. It feels to me as if God is saying that the only thing I have to do is choose. I can have anything and be anything and all will be put in place for my learning of those choices to come about. That's why I have a very deep respect for my thoughts, words and deeds these days. Every one of them has an impact on the whole. They are energy, they are powerful and they potentially affect my and everyone else's quality of life, including that of the natural world. So wherever possible I choose to respond rather than react. I choose to check in to my inner guidance, my higher self, the divinity within. Of course, I'm human and a work in progress, so when I catch hold of a thought that is not in alignment with my higher self I catch and release any energy attached to it. I forgive myself and rectify it with a positive intention. For me, it's about being constantly present with myself and others. Being mindful and compassionate helps, too. I guess it reminds me of the difference between a live show and one that is recorded and edited before being shown.

I love 'going live', as I call it. Often, when I offer up workshops or dialogues with people, within minutes I will sense that whatever it was that we thought we were there to work on disappears and something else magically offers itself up. I love to grab these opportunities to work with that and go for the insights and healing.

This happened many times at Findhorn, and I really enjoyed the times when facilitators or individuals went with it and allowed an issue that may have previously been deeply buried to rise up to be worked with. Sometimes, people would automatically go for an instant shutdown. However, with encouragement, support and often a realisation that it affected more people than just the initiator, it would, more often than not, be engaged with and a healing opportunity would be achieved for all. For me, it is never just about the healing of one individual. Of course, I honour the beauty of one's own healing, but for me it is bigger than just that. When we heal ourselves, we are aiding the healing of the whole; whatever we do ripples out and touches other beings, our planet and the Universe. I believe it has infinite potential.

Sometimes, I would have felt selfish about healing myself when perhaps another would benefit from a different action. Two examples from my social and working background back this up for me.

Firstly, I'm reminded of air travel. There is always an emphasised instruction at the beginning of a flight: in the case of an emergency and the oxygen masks cascading down, you are told, 'Fit your own mask before helping another, even a child.'

Secondly, having attended many 'First Aid at Work' courses, I remember being told, 'Make an assessment of the area you are stepping into with regard to your own safety before offering help to another.' I remember particular instructions: to check for any potential hazards relating to electricity, gas, water or chemicals; to be aware of objects or building parts that could fall on you or give way beneath you.

On one hand, I can see that following through those instructions is a logical choice. It makes sense. After all, if you don't follow the instructions regarding the masks, you could potentially lose consciousness before fitting the mask on another. Consequentially, you could both suffer. Alternatively, you could respond to a cry for help and, in your stepping into the building without due care and attention or waiting for the 'professionals', you could both perish. However, I'm sure many of us will also have witnessed occasions on which those instructions have been ignored and miracles have happened. As a symbolic message, this has often presented me with a quandary, particularly within relationships and, more profoundly, within my family.

I'm interested in playing with the concept that, as a soul, I decided many things before I came here. When and where I would be born, who my parents were going to be and what my purpose was. These factors would offer me the greatest opportunity to heal, transform and achieve the greatest good for myself, for those around me and for this planet. When I accepted this as a concept, I noticed a shift within me from victim to someone who was willing to take personal responsibility for her life. I began to see the gifts within and around my previous experiences in life, rather than their challenges. This enabled me to see where I was being guided or carried rather than where I thought I was abandoned.

When we are born, all the agreements, contracts and our purpose/mission are generally wiped from our memories. Often our natural gifts and talents, such as access to our body wisdom, psychic ability, telepathic communication with all beings, spirits and nature and our connection to Source and oneness, become latent. I say 'often' because I have had childhood experiences and have heard of others where some of our wisdom plays out, yet is dismissed by the people around us. As adults and elder siblings, we often imagine that we know better. As a young child, we can think that we have no option but to accept that this is the case. We begin to disbelieve ourselves and sometimes become fearful, even shut down from some of the things we have access to. We will have been told that we are telling lies, making up stories or imagining things. Responses to food are often described as likes and dislikes and sometimes we can be punished for not eating what is put in front of us. How many of us have heard the one 'there are thousands of children starving in Africa; now eat up'? Although I am eternally grateful to be told that thousands were dying in Africa and want to play any part I can in wiping out that type of poverty and deprivation, I didn't think drinking milk and eating tinned carrots or stewed kidney was going to assist. Couldn't they see that if they continued making me drink my milk and eat other dairy produce then my health was going to suffer? That tinned carrots did not contain all the wonderful things that fresh or organic food does? That eating the organs or flesh of a dead animal is not best for everyone? Fortunately, these days there is much more of an emphasis on 'You are what you eat'. For my part, I didn't have the capacity to explain to my parents and teachers why I couldn't. It was just something I knew. Would they have listened if I could explain it? All I could say was that I didn't like it.

So for many years I would suffer with nasal and chest problems, none of which I have suffered from since giving up dairy products at the age of fifty-one. At the same time, I chose to eat organic wherever possible and I also gave up eating meat, fish and wheat.

Some children will have had and continue to have contact with angels, the fairy realm, spirits and guides. Some will have seen auras and will be fully cognisant of psychic and telepathic powers. As a child I chose to give my power away and it took me a long time to regain it. I lost my self-worth and self-trust and generally lost respect for those around me; I felt they were wrong because they were not open, understanding or accepting of who I truly was. And in turn I became less understanding of who they were. I became someone else in order to fit in. It was my first compromise and it was a no-win situation. I still didn't fit, it seemed.

I would encourage parents, guardians and teachers to be more open to the wisdom of children. We have a lot more sensitive children (Indigo and Crystal children) than before around us at the moment. They need our understanding and acceptance. They have gifts and talents which are of benefit to us and they wish to share them. They may talk to us about the beings that are in their lives that we might not be aware of: fairies, angels, spirits, mermaids, unicorns or ascended masters. They may talk about auras and colours surrounding people, animals and plants. They have the ability to tune into another's feelings and needs. It will often appear that they can guess what you want them to do or what you need, such as a cuddle, a drink or the telephone directory. They know the truth and often can't understand when adults around them lie. We may call it a white lie, but anything other than the full truth is a lie to them. They will also notice when we are untruthful with ourselves.

The greatest potential for support will initially come from their parents or guardians. It will be up to them to hold a loving space so that these children may share their information and experiences. They don't expect you to know the answers or even have the same abilities. They need you to accept and work with them so that they may develop themselves and share their gifts and talents to serve the highest good.

Often, if they are not nurtured and held in a space of love, which can require a lot of one-to-one attention, they can become diverted and either shut down or act out inappropriately. They may even turn to drugs, alcohol or other forms of self-sabotage.

Indigos in particular will push the boundaries and are psychic. Often they are mislabelled as ADHD (attention-deficit hyperactive disorder). Crystals are often calmer and quieter and will often speak at a later stage than other children. It isn't that they are slow in developing; it's just that they don't know that they need to communicate in that way. They were already communicating telepathically and were not aware that others couldn't. There are also some older children, even adults, who were early Indigos and Crystals. They came to pave the way, to help support the influx of sensitives that are being born and to support the parents of those children in any way that they can.

As a child, growing up, I felt separate from my biological family. It seemed that I was different. I felt I'd been taken home from hospital by the wrong parents. They must have mixed up the records, I remember thinking, or maybe I'd been abducted. To my remembering, my parents didn't act as I thought my parents would. They didn't touch, kiss, cuddle or play with me in the way I'd imagined. Something used to happen in my bedroom at night and to this day I don't have a clear idea of what that might be. I just remember every night searching every nook and cranny to see if anyone was there. Even the smallest drawer would be opened. This was a ritual that I carried throughout most of my life whenever I was alone in my bedroom. It even happened one night when I was at Ruskin aged fifty. A few months before I went there, I heard an angel speak to me just as I was about to go to sleep, and she said that no harm would come to me.

That night at Ruskin, I had awoken from a deep sleep and went to the loo. When I came back into my study/bedroom, still in a sleepy state, without thinking I opened my wardrobe and started searching. All of a sudden I was brought to my senses and I realised that I didn't have to do this any more. There was nothing for me to be afraid of. Any contact with me now was only from a loving source and I was protected.

I remember thinking as a child that the house we lived in was wrong, too. I always felt more distant from my mother than from my father. In fact, I can only remember one occasion when I felt close to my mother. I was a young teenager at the time. We were decorating my bedroom together and I remember laughing with her. It felt so good. I can even feel it now. It can't have been much fun for my parents, having a child who appeared to be questioning their way of being all the time and in some way reinforcing or generating the distancing. It may have been interpreted as defiance. I would often have this air about me that things were not good enough. I never wanted to go to places like Littlewood's for a cup of tea and would play up when taken there. I would say the cups were not clean enough and I would always find the one with the crack in. I think maybe I was more used to the 'silver tea set brigade' in a previous life. It must have been difficult for all of us, I think, even my brothers.

My parents must have had some happy times, but I seem to have chosen to remember only the bad times, particularly the arguing. I would lie awake with my door ajar so that I could listen to every word. I never liked the silences. During those times I was always on tenterhooks, waiting for what was going to happen next. For years I would always jump if someone spoke in a loud voice or there was a bang. Silences continued to panic me and often I would fear the worst, whether that be from a parent, teacher, friend, lover, husband, manager. It's not surprising, then, that I have resisted silence for most of my life, always fearing the worst in its presence. It might explain why years later I would want to reject Eileen Caddy's, one of the co-founders of the Findhorn Community, calling to silence in order to connect with the voice within. I would often be touched by sad memories in silence, too. So that's probably why I would always have either the television or the radio on when I was doing my homework or in the house on my own. It wasn't until I went back to studying as an adult and started to do some work on my book that I began to feel comfortable in silence. Obviously, I had learnt to appreciate its value through meditation and visualisation. I had learnt that this was where my prayers could be answered and insights would come to me. It was also where I was able to connect with Source and feel the oneness. Slowly, I'm beginning to integrate that connection without having to go into the silence. To be in a place where Spirit can work through me on a second-by-second basis.

As well as the silence, I often felt quite frightened because I could sense what was going on between people. I felt a lot of anger and sadness. There didn't seem to be any connection between us. Not the bonding that I was expecting. I felt like an unwanted package. This stuck with me throughout my childhood. I would witness what was happening within the family dynamics and feel it was wrong. Yet I had no idea of what 'right' might look like. I judged them for it, and myself, too, not realising that they were doing their best. I didn't appreciate them for that until a short time ago.

It was only a year or so ago, when I was doing some research for my book, that I contacted the people who lived in the house where I grew up. I was so surprised at the response I received. I wrote and posted the letter on the Monday, returned home on the Tuesday evening to find a message to contact them on my answerphone and was visiting them on the Thursday. I certainly felt that I was meant to be making this visit. Can you imagine receiving a letter from a stranger asking if they were able to come into your house and visit all the rooms and garden in order to do some research for their book? The couple were wonderful and I will never forget their generous offer to visit and the welcome they gave me.

Before the appointment, I had spent some time visiting old haunts in the village and 'tuning in' to the area. It was a sunny evening, so I sat beside the river Thames, where I had often played with my brothers and friends. I was contemplating why I had come and what I was expecting to find. Half of me wanted to see if I could connect with what made me feel so frightened in my bedroom, and the other was looking for a sense of completion. 'Putting some ghosts to rest' was the phrase that came to mind. I was remembering my theatrical exit, aged seventeen. At the time, I had felt angry, isolated and unloved. Slamming the door, uttering an unrepeatable phrase aimed at my mother, I vowed never to return again. I remember the house shaking behind me as I stormed off. Now I wanted to know what it would feel like to go back.

While sitting there, I watched the river gently flowing, people on their boats, families playing ball games, dogs searching for the thrown stick and lovers lying in the grass. The sun's rays were warming my bare arms and my pen flowed with all my feelings cascading onto the page. The essence of those feelings was that the past is the past and the only thing to centre on now is the present. Being in the now, releasing dramas, letting everything pass through me. I felt refreshed and renewed. I realised I also wanted to 'tune in' to the house to see if I could pick up anything psychically. I began to wonder how I might do that without disrespecting the family I was visiting. Usually, I like to sit quietly and focus on what's around me, but I thought I might get a few funny looks and maybe a request to leave. As usual, I thought the best thing to do was to play it by ear.

I had been there less than five minutes when I knew it was OK to share with them some of the things I did for a living. I think I used the phrase 'energy work' when asked what I did. I was then asked if I did readings or medium work. When I said 'yes', the response I got was:

'Oh, I believe in that, too. I'm glad you came, because we have something funny going on in the main bedroom.'

They didn't use it themselves, apparently, and when visitors came they found it hard to sleep there and noticed lots of 'odd things happening'. So the way had been cleared for me to do what I needed to do for myself, and in exchange I was able to connect with the woman's brother who had passed over and I did some angelic light work in the bedroom they referred to. It was while the husband was talking to me about one of their children's experience with the 'white lady' that I told him that I had seen her too. I went on to tell him that when I was little and skipping I had seen her in the alleyway between the houses.

'That's where my daughter saw her, too.'

The funny thing is that until I spoke those words I had no previous recollection of that experience. That part of me had been awoken by the visit. I wondered if as a young child I had been so frightened that I had decided to shut down. It was to be forty or so years later when I reactivated that part of me. I also discovered that their child who had seen the 'white lady' had in fact had a poem published herself, which was why, I believe, they were so open to allowing me into their home as part of my research for this book.

I left the house feeling very blessed. Blessed to have followed my guidance to reconnect with the house, blessed to have been received so graciously and to have had the experience I had. Having released outcomes, their graciousness far exceeded anything I would previously have expected. It was also an example to me of an instance where the highest good of all was being served. We all got something from that experience, which I believe was why it flowed the way it did.

It felt to me that as a family we could benefit from some healing. My parents, it seemed, were unhappy living with each other. There would be times when one would leave, come back, the other would leave and so it would continue. An unsettling time for all. I don't remember talking to my brothers about it. In fact, all three of us have said at different times how little we remember of our childhoods. But at some stage we must have agreed to come back and be together for some positive purpose, so I continually look for insights into that and what my part is.

I married before I was to be reconciled with my mother; she declined an invitation to come to the wedding, which seemed fair enough to me at the time. My father was insistent on coming and thankfully brought my two brothers with him. I was a couple of months off being nineteen when I married. I really didn't want to. It wasn't a healthy relationship for either of us, but at the time I felt I had no choice. 'Why didn't I trust myself?' was a question I often used to ask myself. As my wedding day drew nearer, I developed sciatica and could hardly move. I knew I would be OK, though, because I'd seen the movies – the father of the bride always asked the bride if she wanted to go through with it. I'd seen it happen many times. I would fall weeping into his arms and be rescued. He didn't ask me, though, and I never said a word. As a married couple, we did have some good times together but a lot more not-so-happy experiences. We lost our first baby when I was three months pregnant but went on to have two beautiful boys. We separated when our youngest was three months old.

Many years later, after returning from Croatia, I had this idea to arrange a visit to meet up with my deceased father's sister. She is his only remaining sibling. I had no idea why I was doing it. It was another one of those intuitive experiences which I had decided to follow. Although we hadn't spoken since my father's funeral, I had a lovely conversation with my aunt when I phoned. She was a bit surprised to hear from me, as it had been a while. I remember her response: 'Oh, it's lovely to hear from someone in the family after all this time. And it's not about someone dying.'

During the visit, my aunt had some photographs she had found to give me. It was only as I was looking at my parents' wedding photograph that I noticed that my father's mother and father were not there. It felt sad to see that. I was also surprised when my uncle told me how besotted my father was with my mother. Apparently, he and my father had been working together when my parents were courting. It filled my heart to hear of those happy times. It made me wonder if I had been conceived through love, even though it might have been a bit of a shock – my choosing to arrive so early in their courtship. I suppose the photograph explained why my father was adamant about attending my wedding and why he may not have asked the question I was hoping he would. It set me wondering, why my mother had felt she couldn't come to my wedding. What was the pain for her? It must have been huge, I'm imagining. It also kept her away from my brothers' weddings and my sister-in-law's funeral. The next time I was to see her at a family event was at my young brother's funeral. She did try to come to me then, but I couldn't receive her. My pain was too great at the time. Not just because of my brother's death, which was huge in itself. I was angry and in my own pain. I had wanted that touch for such a long time, yet I resisted by saying, 'Not now, Mum.'

I had always dreamed of her ringing me up or turning up at the door and being swept up by loving arms. At the time, I didn't want to think that it took my brother's death to bring us together. I wasn't in a space to see that such a sad act of fate could offer an opportunity for healing. I needed to be wanted in my own right; 'not on the back of my dead brother' was how I put it at the time.

This was why, when I was looking for my son, I realised it was my turn to hold out an olive branch.

What was becoming clear for me was that we had some patterns showing up in our family and it was time they stopped. There was a lot of pain and separation. It was time for some healing to take place.

When I was divorced from the children's father, it was agreed that the children would remain living with me. This they did until my elder son was around twelve, when he decided he wanted to go and live with his dad and stepmother. He said he wanted to live in a proper family with a mummy and daddy. I didn't want him to go, but how could I keep him there when he was begging to go elsewhere? There was also a ghost hanging around in the shape of my attempted suicide. As the children were young and away with my brother at the time, it was assumed that they were unaware of what happened. However, when my elder son came out with his request, I did wonder if he knew or guessed. But how could I put that to a twelve-year-old?

'Do you want to go because I attempted suicide? Because if that's the case I can guarantee I won't do anything like that again. Please don't go. I promise you will be safe and looked after. I love you so much.'

I never spoke those words, but after speaking with his father and stepmother he went to live with them. I really can't speak with authority about what exactly happened over the next four years, but the relationship between them deteriorated. My son rang me one Sunday morning to say his father was throwing him out there and then. Apparently his father had come to the end of his tether and it was a case of his marriage or his son. It wasn't long before I realised I'd picked up a runaway horse. Our family reunion didn't go as well as I had hoped for. There was a lot of sibling rivalry, to put it mildly. I was still recovering from my depression and had formed a new relationship. The long and short of it was that my elder son drew the short straw again. I'd asked for external help from support agencies in keeping the family together. Apparently, there were no resources available for that type of work in our area, but there was a place in a children's home.

'That is out of the question' was my first reaction.

My son said that he wanted to have a look. So we explored it.

'Well, it's a definite no,' I said when we returned.

However, he was adamant that it was what he wanted. How does a sixteen-year-old choose that as the best option? Needless to say, he went to live there. The years would roll by and there would be times when either his father or I would set him up in different bedsits. At the time, he had little or no self-reliance. He had no experience of managing money, positive relationships or work experience. So the opportunities would fail. He would nearly always lose his home because the rent wasn't paid or he had other people living there, which was against the rules.

From an early age, my son had never really liked being on his own, especially in the dark. I feel this is why he gravitates to people, and if you are out of work with little or no money and want to block that out then you will attract like-minded people. They would become his company. His father or I would get the odd phone call every now or then and would share the news of him. Eventually, we lost all contact, but the two years when there was nothing were very difficult for me. I never doubted for one moment that he would be living anywhere but in Plymouth, but there was no letter or phone call. I would make frequent trips to Plymouth, leaving letters at various agencies that I thought he might come into contact with. I would leave up-to-date information about me and also a request to call me if he wanted to. I discovered much later that he never got any of those letters. I would also speak to young people who were begging or selling the Big Issue to see if anyone knew him. Again, nothing. I have to say, I never met with any negativity from either the agencies or the people I connected with. People always seemed to be as helpful as they could be with me and they all wished me luck.

After two years, I got this energetic connection with my missing son. I was living in Findhorn at the time. I followed my intuition and sought out a woman, also a member of the community, whose name came to me. I discovered that among many things she was psychic. When I turned up at her door, she was wonderful.

'I know you can help me,' I said. 'I don't know how, but when I got a message about my son this morning I was also told that I was to come and see you.'

I remember her warm smile as she welcomed me in and sat me down. After a moment or two, she said she knew how she could help. Cutting a long story short, what she did was reconnect me with my psychic abilities. Through this reconnection I was drawn to different organisations and people and was even guided to send a letter to a particular newspaper. I found him. I can never thank enough all those people who helped open doors that had been previously closed.

Even though I had the address, finding it was still a bit difficult. It was in the part of the town where nobody knows anyone or where they live. I had walked past a block of flats when for whatever reason I was drawn to look up at a particular window. There was no name on the building, but there was something about it that just winked at me. I was to find out later that the flats had recently been repainted and the sign indicating the address had yet to be replaced. The flats also had a call button on the outer door and no matter which button I pressed no one answered. Eventually, someone came out, so without making eye contact I just reached for the door.

'Thank you,' I murmured, and I was in.

Nobody answered when I rang the doorbell to the flat, so I decided to sit and wait. I'd waited two years and driven from the north of Scotland to Plymouth. I was happy to wait as long as it took. Eventually, two people came up the staircase; as they went to go into the flat, I introduced myself and asked if they knew when my son would be home, as I had reason to believe he lived there. They told me that they hadn't heard of him! I told them I'd be waiting anyway. I waited patiently, sitting on the concrete staircase. After an hour or so, someone came out from the flat to speak to me. After I shared a few bits of personal information about my son with them, I guess they realised I was who I said I was. It was to be a couple more hours before my son returned. The people who my son was staying with were debating whether they ought to tell my son I was there before he came in. I respected their concern and said that I would support whatever decision they made. They decided not to say anything.

After all the things he has been through, I'm not surprised that his energetic antenna is so alert. As he walked me to my car later, he informed me, 'I thought something was going on from the moment I walked into the flat. But I never guessed for one moment that it would be anything to do with you.'

'Ma! What are you doing here?' were his words as he came towards me with his open arms.

Time seemed to stand still. I was so relieved I was getting this reaction. I'd had a lot of time both on the journey down and while sitting on the steps to wonder if I'd done the right thing. In my letters, I'd put out a request for him to get in touch with me if he wanted to. Now I was here without waiting for his answer.

The previous day, while still in Scotland, I had received a call on my mobile from someone who had seen the open letter I had put in the Plymouth newspaper. The woman's voice told me the name of the block of flats where she thought my son was living. She refused to give me the number of the flat, though. That didn't worry me. The haystack was getting smaller. I knew I'd be able to find him now. I was also over the moon at the quick response. As I was leaving the shop where I'd taken the call, I bumped into a young friend from Findhorn. I was so emotional that I felt I needed to tell someone my news and just blurted it out to her. She was thrilled for me, but I noticed her face change as I said I thought maybe I ought to wait to go to Plymouth to find him. After all, it wasn't just a bus ride away, and what if he didn't want to see me?

'I know you'll know what to do,' she said, smiling. She gave me a hug and went on her way. I set off walking towards the sand dunes and offered up a prayer for guidance. I hadn't been walking for more than a minute when it hit me like a bolt of lightning.

'Go now' was what I heard.

Right, I thought, what I want to do next is find the three people I need to inform before I leave. I bumped into two while walking to my car, and I received their blessing and was told to drive safely and keep in touch.

By the time I got back to my room at Cluny, it was late afternoon. There was still a third person I needed to contact. He appeared in the corridor as I was writing a note for him, and so did one of my best friends. She could see something was going on and asked if I needed any help.

'I need you to come with me while I pack,' I said. 'I need someone calm to map out my route and check that I'm packing all I need.'

She was brilliant. Within the hour, I was on the road. I was determined that I wasn't going to stop till I got into England. I knew that would probably be a four-and-a-half hour drive away. There I'd find somewhere to stop for the night and make the rest of the journey in daylight. While travelling down to Plymouth, I received five further calls in response to the letter about my son. Yet still I wondered if I'd crossed a line. The only thing to do was ask.

'Look, son. I can see this is a bit of a shock for you. It's been a while. And I knew I was going to turn up today, but you didn't. You were not prepared for this. It's your call. If you want me to go, I will. If you want me to stay, then that's OK, too. I can stay as long as you need or I can go back today. How do you feel?'

I was glad he was taking a moment to consider it.

'It is a shock, Ma. I did get a letter from you; it came via an agency yesterday. I was going to reply.'

It was then that he told me that I had a three-year-old grandson. His friend had already told me. It felt different somehow when my son told me. It was real now. He was showing me his photograph. He was beautiful.

'Ma. I do want to see you. But I think I need to get used to the idea a bit. Maybe we can chat over a cuppa and then meet up in a day or two.'

'Sounds good to me, son.'

Within two days I was meeting up with him again, and also with my grandson. It was a bit strange getting used to being a nanny to a three-year-old. As I followed his dad up the stairs to the maisonette where my grandson lived, I heard a squeal of delight – 'Daddy, Daddy.'

'Look who I've brought with me,' my son said as he moved to one side.

'Nanny,' he yelped, as I bent down to receive his hug and kisses. Looking at my family, I thanked God I had heard the call.

It was during the lead up to locating my son that I received another spiritual nudge.

'What about contacting your mother? Why not walk your talk? Be the example that you want your son to follow.'

Although there had been some previous attempts at reconnecting with her, they had not been sustainable. Eventually, when my sons were still quite young, I had decided it was time to let go. It was the writing of the letter to the newspaper that triggered the idea for me. I was asking for my son to contact me, so what better way could there be for me to ground that message than for me to contact my mother? I have to say a big thank you to Marshall B Rosenberg, PhD the founder of Non violent (compassionate) Communication. I'd come across his work a couple of years previously and had joined practising groups to work with the format. It seemed such a beautiful way to communicate with other people and with myself. I used his techniques in writing the letters to my son and my mother.

After the reunion with my son, I returned to Scotland to discover that I had a letter waiting for me from my mother. I couldn't believe it. We exchanged a couple more letters before I wrote to let her know that I was going to Croatia to live for a few months. In the letter I asked about the possibility of our meeting up before I went. She had told me that she was going to be away on holiday, so I had no way of knowing if she would receive the letter before I was to leave. However, I did put my mobile phone number in the letter, just in case. I then released any expectation of outcome. I had learnt that this was the best way for me to function in any situation. My way of being now is to surrender control and know that whatever the outcome it will serve the highest good of all.

Before my departure, I was touring the south of England,

visiting friends, when my mobile rang early one Friday morning. As I picked it up, I saw the name 'Mum' appear on the front of the phone to indicate who was calling. I had only punched the number into the memory card a few days before. I was stunned, pleased and peaceful all at the same time. It wasn't surprising, I suppose, for those different parts of me to be present.

'Hi, Mum,' I said.

How many years had it been, I wondered, since I'd last said those words?

There seemed to be a surprised silence from the other end. I'm not sure that modern technology had caught up with Mum yet, and I guess she was expecting to announce herself. Before any words were spoken, a thought went through my head. I was appreciating the love and courage it must have taken for her to pick up the phone and dial my number. I had put the ball in her court with regards to phoning by putting out the request, and she had said 'yes' by making the call. We are still in contact, have seen each other several times now, and although, from my perspective, the relationship is still a little strained, I feel there is some progress being made. I'm refraining from asking all the questions I think I want answering, as I'm balancing it with being in the now. Appreciating what is taking place now. For me, there is healing, so it seems that my prayers for that are being answered.

In one of the letters I received from my mother, I discovered that her father had died when she was very young and that when times were hard it wasn't always possible for her to live with her mother.

Oh my God, I remember thinking, healing our lineage is wider than I first thought.

Originally, I was looking at it as a three-generational happening. I was separated from my mum. My son was separated from both his father and me at various stages. My son's father was separated from his biological father at an early age and was later adopted by his stepfather, although he always refers to him as 'Dad'. Now it had moved out to five generations! Added to that list now was my grandson, who was separated from his father, and my mother, who was telling me that the same thing had happened to her.

This just has to stop, I thought.

How much further back could this pattern go and how might it continue if nothing was done now? As I was the one with the information, it felt as if it were up to me to do what I could. I had no experience of how to do this, so I did as I always do in these situations: I turned to what I describe as 'intention'. I do believe that if the intention is right, comes from the heart and is for the highest good of all then it will be honoured and answered. From that time on, I focused my intention of healing the family relationships between those members of my family who were currently alive, those who had passed over and those who were to come. I was inviting new souls to come for a different learning. This family was cleaning up its act. If there was any chances that my son would be able to reconnect with his son and have a sustainable loving relationship, I wanted to do everything I could to support that if it served the highest good of all. I was even visualising him with his grandchildren. I did not want to limit the extent of the healing. I wanted to invite it in on all levels and for all directions of time.

I'm happy to say that since that time things have definitely been moving. Since then, there have been shorter gaps of time when contact between my son and myself has lapsed due to his current lifestyle. It feels very different, though. I've shown him that it is possible to track people down if you want to, and I realise that as an adult his journey is one that only he can make. I do thank God for the Internet, though. I'm able to put his name into the local Plymouth newspaper website and pick up any stories referring to him. The good news is that my elder son is exploring how different life might be for him. How that might shape up is still embryonic. Throughout all the dark times, I have always been able to see the light flickering away inside him. It never died or dulled so much that I couldn't see it. It seems to be burning a little brighter now. He has so many gifts and talents to share with the world. As he continues along this path, my prayer is that he will begin to recognise them for himself and hopefully that will lead him to another turning point.

A couple of hours prior to hearing some news about my elder son, I received a phone call from my younger. He said that if I were to get a call from his brother, he would be happy to come with me to visit him. I couldn't believe what I was hearing. All I knew was that yet another prayer of mine was being answered. I prayed that there would come a day when I would be sitting around a table with both my sons again: something that had not happened for quite some time.

It was then that I started laughing. Spirit does make me chuckle sometimes. When I had sent out the prayer, I hadn't imagined that the table might be in a prison visiting room. However, it was good enough for me right now. It was a stepping stone to the family meal we would be having one day. I would be with both of my sons and their families.

It was later that evening when my elder son rang me from prison to say that he had received a reprieve for a couple of days. The judge had asked for a report to see if there was any option open to him other than passing on another custodial sentence. Another miracle had happened. I couldn't remember the last time I had spoken to both of my sons on the same day. We were definitely drawing closer together energetically and geographically. At the time, we were the closest we had been for a long while: one son in Bristol, one in Maidenhead, and me in the middle in a small village on the outskirts of Swindon.

I believe my sons also came to give me the gift of love and oneness. I learnt the joy of growing people. In pregnancy, I would cradle my stomach every day, knowing that a life was growing inside me. I would check with the books to see how much they would have grown, how all the different parts of them would be developing. I would talk to them about how much I wanted them to be part of my life and how I already loved them. Many years later, when I was learning to meditate, it would be the visualisation of their faces and the magnitude of that love that brought me close to what I call Source. When I felt alone and was asked to write a love poem while on my creative writing course, it was the thought of my younger son's twenty-first birthday that connected me with that loving place. I suppose that's why I still love being part of the 'growing-people business'. They had chosen to be born, to grow, to develop, and that's why I love working with people and organisations that want to do that too. Although my body has changed through age and is no longer used for growing babies, it now grows ideas and opportunities instead and I love that part of me. So I nurture those ideas as I would my unborn child. I give them the chance of life and watch how they grow. Experiencing that love has led me to loving myself more deeply; a relationship that is blooming and growing as I write. I remember waking one day feeling so in love with life: not only life in general, but also in love with my life. I felt so close and intimate with myself, as if I knew myself inside out. The feeling you get when you wake up with a lover. When you have touched every part of them and they of you. When you reach that crescendo. Sometimes I feel that close to Source and, having been there, I know I am loved: something I would not have imagined I would have felt in this lifetime. I have learnt that in past lives I experienced dying without knowing the love that others had for me. I felt the sadness and the loss as if it were happening in this lifetime. So I decided to heal that pattern, and I'm grateful to Source for the love I feel.

I am also feeling closer to my brother. For my part, I had always 'sat him on my shoulder', not doing anything without thinking about what his reaction would be if I did this or what he might say if I did that. It stopped me doing some things, and at other times I just waited for the sting in the tail. About a year ago, I decided it would be of benefit to both of us if I released that image of my brother as my judge. Guess what? Since that time, he has not appeared to react in that way and I have not felt anything but love for him or from him. At times it even seems as if we are speaking the same language. I realise now that it was never anything to do with him. It was my responsibility, and I'm so glad I eventually discarded my old way of thinking. I feel freer and I'm hoping that he does too. I can't help wondering if the sibling healing between my brother and me rippled out and energetically helped the healing situation a generation down, between my sons. I realise that I now feel part of a family, no longer a stranger in their midst. A family that up until now had been fragmented for aeons. I'm very grateful to Source and the helping guides and spirits that have been helping me in this work. My invitation to you is to never, never be put off doing something because you haven't been on the right course, read the right book or met the right inspirational person. You are all of them. When your intention is for the highest good of all and you are open to insights, synchronicities will surely come your way and you will be guided. There is always support when we choose to heal and work with the light. All that is necessary is working from a place of love. From your heart, centre and trust in yourself. Then you will be guided and know what to do. There is a Sanskrit phrase, *Sarva-antah*, which means everything is inside us.

It might seem strange from someone who offers workshops to others and writes books, but I really do feel there comes a time when each of us needs to take the theories and experiences we've gained and put them into practice. For me, life is my workshop and relationships are my opportunity to heal.

The gifts I've learnt from my younger son are to be truthful with myself and others, to respect the energy of money and to work with boundaries. Being truthful with myself frees me. If I'm cross, disappointed, angry or sad then I speak my truth to the Universe. Often, a trip into nature helps, as the fairies encourage truthfulness and are happy when I free those thoughts. It allows them to bring in new ideas and ways to remedy the situation. I also learnt an enormous amount about boundaries. Both my sons pushed the boundaries and spoke from the heart. My younger in particular seems to have a definite psychic ability in his communications with me, although, in his words, he 'doesn't do that stuff'.

At one time, I wrote to his older brother, saying I hadn't had any news from his younger brother for a while. He had recently moved to Singapore to work. However, I did add in the letter that now I'd said that, I was sure I would hear soon. I received a text from him the very next morning.

One thing I'm very grateful for is that both of my sons have always supported my doing what I need to do and have encouraged me to follow my heart. I think the usual quote is 'I don't understand it, Mum, but if it makes you happy then go for it.'

What more can a mother ask for?

I had spent most of my life thinking I was unlovable. My choice. I own it. I had chosen to step in and out of the roles of victim, rebel and survivor. I had chosen separation. No wonder I was in so much pain. I am beginning to learn what a gift my family is to me. All of my family members. They all bore the gifts of healing. They were offering me love. All I needed to do was to honour their part, receive and examine their gifts to me and choose to heal. I often remind people I work with that gifts don't always come wrapped in shiny paper and with bows. I tell them about some of the gifts I received from my children when they were small. Often they would come running up to me with a beaming face and bright eyes and I would be presented with what might be described as a sticky mess. They would have been off somewhere, wrapping up something that they wanted to give to me; something that usually meant a lot to them. A symbol of their love. Often, it would have been wrapped in newspaper and paste would stick it together. How easily the world can change when I look at everything coming to me as a potential gift rather than a 'slap in the face'. I would also counsel people, letting them know that sometimes a gift comes in the form of a loss. Sometimes we feel that we are losing something: a job, a partner, our home or health. We often try everything we can do to hang onto it. To let things stay the same. We often resist loss and change. If only we could let it go and see it as an answer to our prayers or something that will serve our highest good. We might then have the opportunity to allow something new in.

I have learnt from my own experience that when things appear to be going wrong or are difficult for me to achieve or I feel stuck, I'm probably off track. It is now a sign for me to surrender my current situation to Source. To allow myself to be and to witness the synchronicities that will surely come my way to guide me back on track.

With regards to my relationships with partners, I see now how they too offered to be part of my learning. From them, I have learnt to have respect for myself. To honour my body, my mind, my emotions and my spirituality. I've learnt to stand in my power, to respond rather than react. To choose peace rather than drama and to honour myself and others rather than compromise. I've chosen to release neediness, the desire to please or to rescue. I have learnt to get in touch with my feelings – all of them – and to honour each one of them. I now offer anyone coming into my life the truest me I know and am willing always to revisit that if anything is triggered.

There is no doubt that this joy has been born of pain. So it feels right that I honour and grieve for that which has passed. I grieve for the lost joyful experiences that my family might have shared in. I grieve for the separations, the misunderstandings, estrangements, divorces, deaths, the loss of love and the pain that has been felt within my family. I grieve for the lack of family celebrations, gatherings, mournings when we would have gained strength and comfort from being as one. From being whole. I grieve for the lack of touch, appreciation and intimacy. I grieve the passing of who I was and, while honouring that part of my journey, I celebrate the birth of the woman I am today. I celebrate the connection with my true self – the person I was born to be.

The choice has always been mine: dormant or awake, joy or pain, healing or living in my wounds. I can see the stepping stones I've taken to reach this place. It has taken a while, yet through my learning I have come to believe it is possible for it to happen as instantly as switching on a light. For me, it is in the acceptance that there is nothing but love. Everything else is an illusion. I'm remembering the occasion two years ago when I asked seven different questions over a period of three weeks. Each time, I drew the angel card of 'Acceptance'. Now I see it as the acceptance of oneness, the acceptance of the whole. Unity and community.

So why would a soul choose this journey, this family, this part of the world at this time? Why had I come here, who was I meant to be, what was my purpose? Questions I didn't ask myself until I was about fifty. The answer to the last comes to me in bite-size pieces. The first time I asked my purpose, I was entering a labyrinth on the beach at Findhorn Bay and the answer was very clear: I was here to bring joy and laughter through the release of tears. I smiled at that response. Best start with myself, then, I thought, and I have been gracefully releasing those tears and there certainly has been a lot more laughter in my life. I would say that I am mostly in the presence of joy. The second time I asked the question, the answer was 'to help bring people home', and I thought what a wonderful job that would be. Who wouldn't want to be a beacon – to light the way so that others could fulfil their purpose, too? I guess we are all here to help each other home. To help each other to heal.

With regard to who I am, well, that is unfolding day by day and I pray that it will continue to do so. But the best answer I can give at the moment is that I AM. I sometimes feel like Dr Who's Tardis. The external physical shell may look like me, but inside I'm bigger, more enlightened, more joyous, more grateful, more at one than I've ever been in my life. These experiences have opened up the child in me. The magical part of me. The part where all my wisdom and wonderment are stored. It is from this place that I share this story. A place which I felt would be buried for ever. Who would want to let this vulnerable self arise again after so much hurt and pain? My creativity was crucified, dead and buried. Now it is time for its resurrection. The magic, of course, continues. Life is a miracle. What's more, I'm still growing and continually unfolding.

***** Exercises *****

I would certainly recommend that if you have not yet done any work on your childhood/family/relationship experiences you may want to consider working with another person who is willing to support you. This could be a counsellor or friend. Ask them to hold a space for you while you take a journey to revisit, explore and reframe your experiences. I'm not sure I could have taken my journey without the love of Source or my friends. The following exercises are those that have assisted me on my journey. If you are doing this with a friend, you may like them to ask the questions for you and write down any of the answers you may give.

The following exercise can be done in relation to each family member/person you want to work with (whether they are still on the earthly plane or not) and any 'significant other' with whom you have had a relationship that you wish to heal. You can approach the healing in many ways: on an individual basis or by inviting them all to be in a circle with you at the same time. It's your exercise, your healing, so you get to choose. You may like to do it in 'bite-size pieces', say fifteen to thirty minutes each day, take a couple of hours once a week or dedicate a weekend to it. Choose what would honour your journey the best. I would encourage you to ground the experience in whatever way suits you: journaling, voice recording or any other creative expression that will serve you.

Be sure that you have uninterruptible time to do this. Imagine yourself in a warm, safe space. Feel the beauty all around you. You might be on a beach, in a wood, by a stream – wherever you would feel happy and safe. Focus on something symbolic which can be placed in the centre of the circle. It may be a piece of driftwood, a campfire, a rose bush. Know that you can always come back to that focus at any stage throughout the exercises. From that place you can reconnect with yourself, your body, the room you are in, and open your eyes. Some people like to have quiet; others prefer some low, gentle music.

Imagine whoever you have invited to sit opposite or in a circle with you. Know that they have agreed to be there and listen to you. They will not speak until you ask them to respond. This is your opportunity to say exactly what you feel about what has passed between you. Take time to connect with your true feelings and speak from the heart. Own everything you say. Connect with what you are feeling and express it from a place of I (i.e. I feel, I need). Tell them what your unmet needs are. Take all the time you need to connect with the feeling and the need. If you need to express anger, then let it flow. Many of us suppress anger for many reasons. Rest assured that it will serve your highest good for this to be released. It will pass through the central symbol and be transmuted by the elements to love. If you are feeling bereft, allow those feelings and words to come through; if you are grateful, express that in whatever way you would truly like to, even if that is in a way that wouldn't usually come naturally to you.

When you have released what you need to say or do, try not to censor, judge or blame yourself. Be compassionate with yourself.

When you are ready, invite those present to respond to you. Know that they will be responding from their higher self and you will be receiving what they say and do from yours.

After the exercise, check in with yourself and see how you feel. What changes do you notice within you and around the relationship? Have you reached a resolution? Has something new arisen? Do you want to set another time to go back and revisit that issue? Notice what happens in the future between you and the person(s) you have just connected with. What healing have you witnessed?

The power of prayer, affirmation, intention and communication to and from the higher self. What part do any of these play in your life? What, if anything, holds you back from working with them? What outcomes have you witnessed? If you get something you didn't think you asked for, might you need to look back and reword some of them to ensure you are specific enough and working to the highest good?

How confident are you in following your intuition or your psyche? Do you witness those 'if only I had followed that thought through' moments? Remind yourself to consider your first thought. Try playing with it sometime and following the guidance to see how it can support you. Once you tap into the grid, it's amazing how it will continue to work with you. Maybe even join a development group.

Indigo and Crystal children – this is a huge subject so if you feel you are one of the early arrivals or know someone who is one then take a look at the website I've listed at the back of this book as a starting point.

Rosie

Letting Go and Moving On

ROSIE WAS AND STILL IS IN SOME WAYS VERY IMPORTANT IN my life. For just under three glorious years she was my dear companion and we journeyed far together. The love and appreciation was instant from the moment I clapped eyes on her until the day I had to let her go. Even now, the memories of her just fill my heart. Rosie was my beloved car: a Toyota Corolla, silver, five-door model. She was a real beauty and the newest car I had ever owned. She was very reliable and I appreciated that. Together we covered a fair few miles. We made many trips from the South of England to Scotland and then back down again to the West Country. I'd never had such a relationship with a car before. I'd always appreciated them but had never shared or learnt so much from the experience as I did throughout our time together. References to her will no doubt pop up in other places in this book

It was while I was at Findhorn that I noticed machines were given names, which I thought a bit weird at first. However, as time went by I realised how much more I loved and appreciated them once they were named. It was then that I was more able to value the contribution they made to my life. After all, if I was choosing to work with the concept that 'work is love in action' then why wouldn't I appreciate everything that was helping me in that work? For me, the love and appreciation goes beyond the appliance itself, because someone will have invented, designed, produced, packed, transported and either sold or given the item to me. There is always the opportunity to be grateful to the animal and natural kingdoms for the part they have played, too. I know that in some countries people, animals and the environment are not appreciated or fairly recompensed for the part they play. I'm grateful to the agencies that are active in these arenas. I'm also sure that some energetic appreciation will be gratefully received and aid the process. Allowing my love and gratitude to extend as widely as this gives me the opportunity to witness how many people on this planet potentially touch my life at any given moment. It feels great to be part of that wider community.

Experiments have shown that plants, trees and water react differently when treated and spoken to in a loving way. Dr Masaru Emoto in his books *The Hidden Messages of Water* and *The True Power of Water* shows through high-speed photography that crystals formed in frozen water reveal changes when specific thoughts or prayers are directed towards them. He found that water from clear springs and water that had been exposed to loving words showed brilliant complex and colourful snowflake patterns. However, polluted water or water exposed to negative thoughts formed incomplete, asymmetrical patterns with dull colours. Considering that we humans are approximately seventy per cent water, it is no wonder that we react the way we do to positive and negative vibrations and why they affect our health. Prayer is a great healing tool. I believe that it was those images that prompted me to speak more lovingly to all machines, animals, nature, Rosie and in particular the people in my life. I was mortified at first when I saw his research. I was imagining the pollution I had been responsible for in the past with my negative thoughts, especially to my fellow humans. I could have been a walking Chernobyl, spreading devastation wherever my negative thoughts landed. I have from that time been working as well as I can to clear that karma and to ensure that I am conscious of my thoughts and take responsibility for them. Thoughts can become form. Dr Masaru Emoto proved that. That is a powerful concept, and one that led me to another of my lessons: discernment. Like many of my lessons, I learnt this the hard way, but it has taught me to be wiser and to think of the whole.

Shortly after becoming aware of the power of thoughts, I was attending a football match with a girlfriend of mine. One of the teams we supported had a big match coming up and we headed off to Cardiff to watch them in the play-offs. It was a lovely day and the crowd was really excited. I don't know why it came to me, but I wondered whether the team would get a goal if I could concentrate enough and wish them to play well enough. The thought went in, then out. During the game, I went to the loo, and it was while I was there in the quiet that I concentrated on the team I was supporting getting a goal. Before I had even left the cubicle, a loud roar went up throughout the stadium. Of course, I wouldn't know who had scored until I got back to my seat.

'You missed the goal,' my friend told me. 'We're one up.'

Interesting, I thought. What a coincidence. A while later, another thought came. What if it wasn't a coincidence? What would happen if I did the same thing again? So I trotted off to the loo and concentrated. Up went another roar. When I got back, I discovered we had scored again. It was then that I started to feel a bit uncomfortable. This didn't seem right to me.

As the match was drawing near to the end of full time, we were drawing. If there wasn't a goal soon, we would be going into extra time. Out of the blue, from farther down the row, I heard a man's voice shout out:

'Eh, luv, do you fancy going to the loo again? Every time you go, we score.'

By this time the whole row between me and him was staring at me, willing me to go. I decided to treat it as a joke and laugh it off. There was another goal, but it came from the other side and we went home the losers. Life was busy at the time and I didn't think any more about the incident until a while later when a similar occurrence came to face me square on.

I was bringing together the concept of thoughts becoming form and the power of group prayer. At the same time, I was faced with a situation concerning my elder son. He was in prison at the time, awaiting a sentence. It was shortly after I'd reconnected with him. He phoned to tell me that the mother of his son had offered him the opportunity to go and live with them and to see if they could support him in coming off drugs and become a family. This seemed like a golden opportunity to try out my new-found theory. I emailed everyone in my address book, texted everyone in my phonebook and put a photograph of my son on the noticeboard in Findhorn, where I was living at the time. I was asking people to send positive thoughts or to pray for him over the next couple of days as he had the opportunity to be reunited with his family. It felt at the time as if it were coming from a pure place. It was the evening before his appearance in court when I thought of the judge. I realised that I'd asked everyone to concentrate on my son, but not on the judge, who was one of the key people involved with the decision making. So I took that task on myself, asking him to use his wisdom to enable my son to be reconnected with his family and have an opportunity to come off drugs. Of course, I received a call the following day and it was my son. He had not been given a custodial sentence, as the judge was releasing him on probation and he would be living with his family. As you might imagine, I was relieved, over the moon. I was walking in the dunes behind Findhorn Bay at the time and I remember holding my arms out wide and thanking everyone for the part they had played.

Within a week, I heard from his partner that it hadn't worked out. Evidently what happened is best told by their truths and understanding. What hit me as a realisation was huge.

Oh, my God! I hadn't considered or included the phrase 'for the highest good of all'.

Could I have been responsible for putting him into a situation that didn't serve him at that time, regardless of whether it was what he wanted? I had written the scenario as if I were writing the ending to a story I wanted to see played out. I had set the stage – scripted the players and prompted the audience, too. It became all too clear that my son needed time to find himself and become a family to himself before being put into the situation of doing so with his then-partner and son. I'd helped set him up to fail. It was a hard lesson to learn and a hard way to learn it.

It was at that moment that I remembered the football game. Regardless of whether the goals and my wishes were a coincidence or not, the learning was plain to see. It needs to be for the highest good of all. That is what this journey is about. That doesn't take anything away from me. After all, I am part of the whole. I am a reflection of the whole. The time has long gone where I would beat myself up for such a realisation. What I choose to do now is to accept the learning. Be grateful for it, forgive myself and live by it. It was a time of letting go. Letting go of my old ways and embracing the new awarenesses that were coming my way. I was adding discernment to my newly forming 'tool kit'.

My reason for telling you about Rosie now is mainly to do with more letting-go situations. I was amazed with the insights I received from releasing her and wanted to share those with you. I will always be grateful for that process and the part she played. I had a sense from the start of my journey that the time would come when I would need to let her go. It was as if it were predestined that I would need to be homeless, moneyless and assetless in order to learn many of my lessons. I'm not saying that we all need to learn that way or even that I had to learn that way. I accept that it was an opportunity for me to work with it at that time, and I chose to say 'yes'.

So here I was in August 2005 with some credit card debts; albeit small debts, a couple of hundred pounds. I had no fixed income and no savings when I realised something needed to be done. I'd only recently started to use the cards again and had run up the debts for two main reasons. Firstly by incurring costs while helping my elder son out with a few things; he needed to go into rehab when I didn't have the money to pay for it. Secondly because I was spending money, thinking that I would generate an income by offering myself as a spiritual coach, mediator and Reiki practitioner. So, I asked myself, what were my lessons?

There was something about releasing the responsibility I felt for my son becoming a drug addict. Also, I was willing to release an old programme of mine where I felt compelled to dash in as the rescuer. I realised that there was a lack of congruence about personal responsibility. If I was accepting that it was up to me to take personal responsibility for my life, knowing that all the way along the line I had choices, then surely the same went for my son. If I believed I chose my parents in order to learn the lessons I needed to learn, then surely the same went for my sons. As I accept that as a truth, I also feel the human pain of potentially harming another being, especially one's own children and loved ones. I know my intention was not to harm. In fact, after my experiences as a child, I wanted everything to be so different for my sons.

At the birth of my elder boy, something got lost during the process. Even now, I still feel I knew what would have been best to happen and this was contrary to the medical advice I received. Although accepting of it now, for many years I was disappointed that I gave in. I was sure that he was going to be born on 25 December, but I was taken into hospital a few days before, as they wanted to induce me. Someone said that it was because they didn't want a rush over the Christmas period. Anyway, I don't think he was ready. Even before they started inducing me, someone suggested that he had disengaged and maybe it wasn't time, but that got overridden, too. It was a long day, but the thought of having my baby in my arms far outweighed the physical and emotional pain I was feeling. I refused all pain relief, as I didn't feel I needed it, but as the time wore on and my baby and I became tired I was asked to accept pethidine. I had previously refused it on three occasions. Eventually, I was persuaded that they knew best; after all, I was a 'new' mum-to-be and they had done this many times. They also said that I should accept it for my baby's sake. They had me there, so I reluctantly agreed. I have no idea why they suggested taking it, because for me it took everything away. I felt like a zombie, no longer part of the process. It was happening to someone else, not me. More than that: it felt as if my feelings were being blotted out yet again in my life. So when the birth finally happened both my son and I were 'out of it'. I'm not saying that all mothers will experience the same effects with the drug, but I can assure you it was definitely not for me.

After the first few minutes of holding my baby and checking him over, he was taken away from me. I felt he was a unique child. He was born jaundiced and because of an 'abnormality' around his crown there was a circle of hair that had grown very long and black, while his otherwise short hair was blond. For me, it just added to his own special individuality. I was told by the doctors that there was no need for concern and that, although they would monitor him for the first year or so, they were not expecting it to have any impact on his life. By the time I had been returned to the ward after being stitched, I was feeling very disconnected from the whole process, and my baby son seemed drugged for days. I can't help but wonder if that start had an impact on his addiction to drugs in later life. It was a few weeks before I felt a real bond to him, but after that the love that flowed was something I had never experienced in my life before. I even wondered how people went on to have more children. I had always wanted to have at least six, but now I wondered how I could do that. To love another, I felt, would be to take away some of the love that this child needed. On reflection, I wonder if there was a truth in that thought.

When I was a teenager, drugs were available among my peers. Not as much as it seems today – well, not from my observations – but it was always something I resisted very strongly. The only reason I can think of was that I wanted control and with drugs I would lose it. I think it would have been a killer for me, especially being an unhappy teenager, to have gone down that route.

For me, here was an insight about trust: trusting my own inner wisdom. When I don't, I can see that I give my power away. Why did I not have faith in my own belief? I need to know that I am wise and know exactly what to do at any given moment. It is still a struggle at times, but I am accepting my own inner and bodily wisdom a lot more than I did before I started this spiritual journey. I have confidence, too, that it will grow and grow. What I carry with me from this life is that as a child it was painful for me to experience being put down all the time. When I was getting messages continually coming to me that I was in the wrong, I began to believe it. When I look back now as an adult, I say 'no' to that message. I was right. It is cruel to force milk down a child's throat; to abuse them with your hand or ruler; to belittle their offerings; to make them so afraid that they lie, fearful of what the truth may bring. It would be similar messages to this that brought me to my deepest depressed state when I attempted suicide. My second marriage was on the verge of divorce; on looking around me, I saw that I was the common denominator and jumped to the conclusion that I must be the 'bad' being – it was my fault. I was the failure. In past lives when I might have spoken my wisdom, I would have been accused as a heretic or rebel and suffered the consequences of being tortured, burned at the stake, hanged or drowned. I suppose it is no wonder that with all this 'baggage' my lesson is so hard to learn. So I am learning to trust myself in all situations and know that I am connected to Source. It is still an interesting and ongoing journey for me, growing closer to the Source within and learning to act from that place. Also to witness and honour it in those around me.

I had wanted my children to have such a loving childhood and *not* to have the experience I had. Again, too late, I realised that the Universe does not understand the word *not*. Far from providing that loving stable family relationship that I had so wanted, by the time my elder son was three and a half and my younger three months old I was separated from and preparing to divorce their father. I believe that every child has the right to have a safe, nurturing, loving and creatively expressive childhood and every parent has the right to have faith that they can be all that their child needs. I often wondered when I was drawn to work with people who requested support with parenting why we didn't learn this as children and young adults. At first, I aimed my disappointment at the education system, and I suppose they would in turn say it is a parental responsibility. It appears more than ever to be a chicken-and-egg situation. From my point of view, it is a collective social responsibility, but as a society we don't generally work in that way. For me, the truest influence and control I have is how I respond to this and any other situation. There is hope, though, for the collective consciousness to work positively. I witnessed this most profoundly with the wave of responses to the tsunami on Boxing Day, 2004. We didn't wait for governments to act or advise us. Individuals acted straight from the heart, from their own consciousness, immediately, in whatever way they felt was appropriate. I saw it as an excellent model of offering our gifts and talents to those who were in need. It is a model I feel most comfortable with. I remember that when I was studying at Ruskin I opted for a module on Marxism. Having no previous understanding of his philosophy, what struck me as an instantaneous truth was, in simple terms, 'give what you can – take what you need'. The philosophy works; it did in the time of Atlantis. The downfall of Atlantis and Marxism is ego. Our ego can take us away from the utopia, away from its beauty. I identify with that when I witness myself or others starting to compare, to judge or to criticise, or when I witness greed, hoarding and a focus on lack rather than abundance. It is then that I move from a place of love to a place of fear.

Unhealed childhoods lead to more negative parenting experiences, which lead to even more negative childhood experiences. I look at what is happening around us currently in society. Now, that is a revealing statement in itself, isn't it? Do I look at what I see or at what is projected via the media or hearsay? If it were the latter, then I would believe that society accepts there is no hope for the younger generation, who are branded as unruly thugs or 'hoodies', or for the so called 'scroungers' and 'down and outs'. For my part, I know lots of interesting, kind, helpful, positive, caring, generous, intelligent, spiritual people of all ages. When I look at what is presented via the majority of the media, what I see is people in pain, fearful, unhealed, who are often rebelling against those who seem to want to separate them even further from the society they already feel marginalised by. They are viewed as spurning society's attempts to include them via parenting, mentoring, training or education and are responding with a lack of discipline, use of violence and drugs, inappropriate sexual experiences, abusive behaviour to themselves and others, non-communication or violent communication; they generally have a lack of self-worth, a sense of non-belonging and no appreciation of their gifts and talents which are a gift to themselves and the world. So what is society? It is all of us. Yes, we can campaign to do things on a larger scale, but the real place change starts from is within. So for me that is about asking myself 'What can I do which will make a difference?' and doing that *now*; not next week or when I have time, but *now*. Mahatma Ghandi told us to be the change we want to see in the world. For me, it's not OK to point the finger out, because if I do then there are three fingers pointing back at me. What I choose to do is identify the inner pain and find the resource to heal. My manifesto states that I will support physically, emotionally, mentally and spiritually the healing of all, and my vision is to do myself out of a job.

My hope is raised with the vast number of people who are connecting with the light at this time on the planet. Also with the coming of the Indigo and Crystal children and the higher awareness of their gifts that is currently spreading across the planet. They can, if we choose to listen, offer us help and guidance as to how a balance may be achieved. We can also tune in to our inner wisdom to play our part. This would have a huge social impact on all the other resources we are now engaged in supplying, such as prisons, probation services, health provision, housing, children's homes, young offender establishments, drug and alcohol rehabilitation centres, women's refuges, homeless hostels, and so the list could continue.

Going back to my elder son, who is one of those marginalised, I was feeling that I was throwing money that I didn't have at something I didn't in my heart feel was going to work. It wasn't his time. He wasn't ready. I knew that, and I had also heard it from someone who worked in that field. The money wasn't going to help him reach the stage of wanting to kick the habit; it was helping me, albeit for a short period of time, to feel that it might be a reality and maybe to free my subconscious guilt. In a way, I feel now that I was buying time with him and I was attaching an outcome and an expectation to that part of his journey. Because of my financial circumstances at the time, I had got to the stage where his letters from prison asking for money were always answered with 'I love you, but I have no money'. Because I was helping him out financially, despite all the words in my letter, over this weekend before he went into rehab, I was giving out a mixed message to both of us. I remember being so proud of him because he was going for it and also very much wanting him to succeed. I wonder if that adds pressure to people on an energetic level. What I know is that he will kick his habit and he will feel love for himself and from those around him. I also know that one day he will have a loving relationship with his son and his grandchildren. He is already a gift to this world, and my heart nearly bursts with the love I have for his beauty. I pray that while I hold that image up as a reflection to him he may one day see it for himself.

The second lesson with regards to my credit card situation, and the more obvious for me at that time, was to wait till I had the money before I spent it. I definitely believe that it is OK having faith that things will follow through, but if there was still a learning to be had, and having invited them all to come my way as I had done, then it was going to override everything. There was obviously a relationship-with-money issue for me. I was born into a family where we were well fed; we had a roof over our heads, clothes, birthday and Christmas presents, furniture etc. We lived in a council house, so my parents didn't own their own home, but on a material front I don't remember being without anything. Both my parents worked, and I do remember that holidays were few and far between, so I guess that after the essentials and a few luxuries were catered for there wasn't much left in the pot.

I have never been a great saver and have usually spent what I have. I remember once as a child finding a shilling in the street (equivalent to five pence nowadays but worth a lot more; in those days it would have bought a large loaf of bread with a halfpenny change). I looked around to see if anyone could have dropped it, but as there was no one in sight I went with my friends to the local shop and bought sweets with it. I remember my mum being furious when she found out. Firstly, she thought it was wrong that I had spent it when it could have belonged to someone. However, when I told her I'd looked and asked her whether I should have taken it to the police, she said she didn't think they would be interested. I wasn't sure that I could have done anything else, so I couldn't see what she was so furious about. Secondly, I wondered if maybe she felt spending so much money on sweets was a waste. I guess if money was tight then I can understand that reaction. I imagine that was what I was witnessing at that young age. I was noticing a reaction and not a response. I do remember the feeling of being rich and being able to buy things for my friends and my family albeit for a short period. As a child, I was rich for that moment.

These days, I like to think that the more I have, the more I have to share. The same goes with any other energy or power. The more I have, the more empowerment potential there is. I remember people saying about my father that if he had two pence then he would give a penny away. I remember feeling proud of him when I heard that, even though it was sometimes said as a derogatory comment. So I guess this issue with money runs in the family until it is healed at Source.

Although it has always been easy for me to give and to share, it was not always easy for me to receive, whether in a monetary way or in a loving way. I suppose I needed to let everything go for me to learn that lesson.

I've always worked hard and earned my own money from an early age. I started with a paper round before school, followed by a Saturday job in a supermarket, a job in the Brylcream factory during the school/college holidays, and then I started my first full-time job the Monday after I left school. With the exception of a few years on Supplementary Benefit when I was a single mum and my children were very small, I have always been employed and paid my way. So what was this challenge I had around money?

Following on from my last relationship split, the money I had was not sufficient for a deposit on a property in the area I lived in, so I decided to rent. Another reason for renting was that I could have an extra bedroom and, as my elder son was about to be released from prison, it offered him an opportunity for a fresh start. It was one he wasn't ready for and he only managed to stay for a week before he disappeared. It would be two years before I located him and was in contact with him again.

The end of the yearly rental agreement on the house coincided with my planning my new venture – one where I could find a way to live and work more holistically. My younger son had decided to live with his girlfriend and, as they didn't want to live in the house I was renting, there was no need for me to keep it. I decided to use the money I had to support myself in finding a new way of living and of being. At that time, like many students, I was penniless and rich at the same time. Rich with the treasures the last four years had brought me, especially the understanding of my true self; rich with my holistic and spiritual awareness, yet penny-poor with regards to cash. I'm currently manifesting a way to amend my thought process around that situation in a way that is congruent with my truth. Writing this book feels part of it. I was also wondering if my new-found determination to become debt-free had been inspired by the huge global force that is working on governments to eliminate debt from emerging nations. Apart from being debt-free, I also wanted to be freelance.

I'm noticing a desire pattern of wanting to be free. Free to spend every day doing something that brings me joy and is of use to myself and the community around me. I want my life and my work to be the same thing and preferably to operate from the same venue. I'm certainly not opposed to travelling or working either in other environments or collaboratively with other people, but I want the freedom to say 'yes' or 'no' and not to compromise. Developing and sharing my gifts and talents is basically what I am choosing to do. What currently brings me joy is writing, and when opportunities present themselves I also enjoy one-to-one healing, facilitating groups, and speaking and mediation work. I love being part of building and growing joyful and peaceful individuals, families, communities and countries and helping to create a peaceful world.

So these were some of the lessons that presented themselves when the release of Rosie was imminent, even if it is only now that they are unfolding to their fullest understanding.

Was I beginning to know why I had been chosen by my sons for their lessons? There were certainly opportunities for them to learn from addictive behaviour, because at last I noticed that about myself. Especially with regard to seeking others' approval, pleasing, rescuing, watching television, shopping and occasional excessive inappropriate use of alcohol. The question which followed now was what I was supposed to learn from choosing my parents. The first thought that came in was 'to love unconditionally and hold the family together'. I totally understand the first part, as I have always found it easy to love my sons unconditionally. In a way, I feel I was born to love them. I haven't always been able to do that with other family members around me or indeed in other relationships. Hold my family together – wow, that was the first time I'd heard that message. It certainly is far from being together either physically or geographically at the moment. Healing it has definitely been in my awareness. It has been my intention since reconnecting with my elder son after the two-year separation to heal my family past, present and future. How exactly that is going to play out I have no idea. What seems important to me is that I hold that intention and hope that as I heal myself it will ripple out from there. I am learning to let go of past perceptions, past truths and past understandings. I am beginning to look at the past with fresh eyes. New insights come in and I am able to reframe and reprogram my past, which has a huge impact on my present and no doubt my future understandings.

Going back to the money issue: as the credit card bills came in, I soon began to realise that what I could afford to pay was quickly wiped out by the interest charges that were accrued on top. It was a vicious spiral and not one that I wanted to escalate even further. I felt really grateful that at the time I was living in the centre of Reading, a large town, with access to buses and trains that were frequent and literally less than ten minutes away. The place I worked in exchange for my accommodation was opposite a train station, too, which enabled me to get to my other job with Mencap in Henley. I needed to put my thoughts into action, so I decided to ring my cousin who had sold me the car to see what price I might get for her. When I asked him the best way of going about selling her, he thankfully said, 'Don't worry about that; leave it to me.'

As the tax and MOT were running out, I handed Rosie over to him, but it was about a month before she was sold and I received the money. The strange thing was that once I had made the decision to sell her, I was at peace. I released all worries and concerns and was able to be again. To be centred and act from a place of now.

On the last day that Rosie and I spent together, I remember enjoying being able to clean her inside and out. Giving her that final polish gave me some time to complete with her. Having a positive completion was something else I'd learnt from my time at Findhorn. In the past, I would often have left somewhere in a hurry or with a bad feeling, so I would be carrying lots of stuff around with me for years afterwards. I would have left bits of my energy in those places, too. What I do now is try to ensure that I collect all of myself up and endeavour to check in to see if there is any unfinished business which I need to take care of before I leave. It may seem a bit daft to be doing the same with Rosie, but it has become a natural part of the process for me. I am still working on doing this effectively. Sometimes I discover that, while I deal with the surface stuff, the subconscious remains there unless I specifically invite it up. I believe I didn't go deep enough with Rosie, because a few days after leaving her with my cousin my grief and loss kicked in. It had been raining hard during the afternoon when I realised that I would be walking home in the pouring rain. My friend, who I worked for, had offered me a lift, but for some reason I felt that I was supposed to take this journey alone. Isn't it amazing how we know these things sometimes? As I stepped outside, it seemed to me as if the rain were an invitation for me to cry, to mourn the loss of Rosie. I allowed myself to cry all the way home. I soon realised that there was more to loss than coming to terms with it. From a logical point of view, I had been able to do that; after all, I would become debt-free, and that made me feel so much lighter. Struggling with the debts had been so draining and took up so much of my time and energy. I knew I would also enjoy the opportunities to do more walking, and I just love train journeys. I remembered too a newspaper article I'd read some time before, which said that for some people it would be cheaper to take taxis to where they needed to go than to own a car with all its additional financial – let alone environmental – implications. I was pleased to be remembering that at this time. What I felt I was being told was that there are two parts to loss: the acceptance and the physical and emotional grieving that needs to take place. I needed to allow my body to feel the loss, to miss the company, to miss the support, to miss the journeys we had shared, to miss her gleaming, shiny silver exterior and her comfy, soft interior. To miss the safety I felt when she was around me, her reliability and her energy. Funnily enough, the thing I had thought would affect me most didn't surface. I thought I might feel trapped without a car, but it seemed that the Universe provided me with such a multitude of options that never crossed that my mind. During this processing, I realised I was letting go of the 'tough guy' image I had often given out to people and myself. I was connecting to my vulnerability and allowing that to surface and become my strength.

When I got home, I wanted to do some further work on grieving. This wasn't just about Rosie, I realised; this was about all the grieving I had failed to do in my life. While taking part in some purpose work at Findhorn, I drew a guidance card which would support my then-purpose; it said 'I am radiant with release' and I seemed to know it instantly as a truth. I was always letting things go, drawing a line under them, picking myself up and starting over again. I very rarely felt that I needed to hold onto a position or possession, although I have had my moments when I have tried to hold on. But there was more to release, I was realising. I'd only released the tip of the iceberg. There were a further nine-tenths that needed some work, and this was what I was about to start on. So I sat there quietly and asked my body what it needed to grieve. It was amazing what came up for me.

I wanted to grieve for the insecurity that I had felt for most of my life; the loneliness; the lack of belonging, lack of fun and play. I wanted to grieve for the times I wasn't understood, appreciated, loved or honoured. I wanted to grieve for the loss of my first baby and to honour her path and her choice. I wanted to grieve for a lost love, the only man I had truly loved. I also wanted to grieve for the passing of a father, brother, sister-in-law and stepmother. At the time of their passing, I had been surrounded by dramas and had been unable to be my true self and grieve in the way I would have wanted. I was always holding myself together, it seemed. Of course, now I can see that it wasn't myself I was holding together. I was holding together my fantasy of me. The unreal I was trying to break away all that time so that I could see the true me, but obviously I wasn't ready to let it go. I remember thinking just before I attempted suicide that I was like a Ming vase that was falling onto a tiled floor. When I hit it, I would be shattered into a thousand pieces. I think maybe I was close to fragmenting and this was what happened when I went into the void. I don't have any recollection of that except a knowledge that when I came back I no longer felt that way. I felt a certain inner strength that came from a knowledge that I couldn't explain. I wanted to grieve for the part of me that had died that day, but I also wanted to celebrate the newness of the me that had begun.

While I was writing this chapter, my youngest stepsister died, and when I heard the news I decided that I wanted to be present with all my feelings as they arose. I can remember saying to friends who asked how I was that I was present, and it felt empowering to hear myself say that. I gave no consideration to how long the process would take or how it would look; it was an opportunity for me to be in the moment. I had weepy times, angry times, times when I wanted to reach out and times when I wanted to be alone with my thoughts. I had times in the silence and times with the voice of Chris James, a fantastic voice healer. I kept hitting the repeat button for his rendition of 'Beloved One'. There were times when my grieving was not just centred on my stepsister, but it triggered past grief and potential grief. I chose not to judge this but to allow it to come through, always thanking my stepsister for the part she was playing. For some reason, it was like her gift to me, and I was grateful. Part of me was also celebrating that she was no longer connected to the body and mind that had constrained her through fear and confusion for most of her adult life. It seemed to add insult to injury when she was diagnosed with cancer. She hadn't chosen an easy path, and it was often difficult to see her gifts and talents, especially for the people who loved and cared for her. For me, it was her humour and directness that brought me closer to her.

It was the day after her passing that she chose to visit me briefly. I've worked psychically and clairvoyantly for a few years and have often been able to give messages to friends and clients from their loved ones and friends who have passed over. Even though I had wanted to connect with her, I hadn't expected her so quickly. I was making some lunch when I felt something that made me look away from the cooker and there she was, standing next to me. She had a huge smile on her face and held about six cigarettes in each hand, saying, 'I can smoke as many as I like now.' I was so glad she had chosen humour to present herself, as it did lighten me quite considerably. I knew instantly what she was referring to.

I felt at that moment as if I had a choice. I could carry on my grieving process the way I was, or I could know that it was complete and that I could communicate with her differently from now on. I was aware later in the afternoon and evening, when I was receiving phone calls from friends, that I was no longer in pain or mourning a loss. I felt everything had been processed. Just before I went to sleep that night, I heard a message which said that I was clear and my body felt empty. I remember thinking that I had been able, with my stepsister's help, to process my grief for her and other past grief in approximately thirty-six hours. A huge contrast to some of the grief I had been holding onto for somewhere in the region of fifty years. I now know my preference for processing.

She has been quite playful since. I wanted to take a pink scarf with me to the funeral, as I thought it would brighten up my dark clothes and pink was also her favourite colour. However, on the day of the funeral, I searched everywhere for my scarf and it wasn't there. When I told my other stepsister about this, she said, 'There is only one person wearing pink today, and that's my sister.' Apparently, she was dressed in a beautiful pink nightgown and the casket was padded with pink satin cloth. I understood then why it was left behind.

At the church, we were led by the minister to the front pew. My stepsister and her father entered first, and I was then left to take up the space by the aisle which was nearest the coffin. I had this feeling that maybe I shouldn't be there and wondered whether her dad or sister wanted to be there. When I looked towards them to see if they wanted me to move, I could see that they were lost in their grief and so released the notion. It was halfway through the service when she appeared again and asked me to budge up, as I was in her seat.

Now I attempt to take time out on a regular basis to get in touch with all my feelings, and when I do I try to do it by recognising one feeling at a time. That way, no one feeling can feel overridden or compared to another. I want each of my feelings to be honoured and to know that it has my undivided attention. Not everything comes up in one go. That's my preference. I have always asked for it to come in bite-size chunks that I can deal with. But from my recent experience I'm only applying this to old stuff, which is getting less and less. There may be tears when spending time with my newly surfaced feelings, but I can guarantee that my sessions always end with me smiling. It seems that no matter where the journey starts from I always return to love. It never fails to take me there. I'm always lovingly escorted home.

My celebrations from selling Rosie were many. First and most important was that I was now debt-free and have continued to live from that place ever since. This has mainly come about because I have been able to exercise my new-found ability to be a gracious receiver. Secondly, I was grateful for all the insights that had been offered up to me and the opportunity to process them. Such as grieving, letting go, detachment, discernment and, most importantly, faith. Thirdly, I was now doing much more walking, which I realised I had been missing, and taking other forms of transport, which I was very much enjoying. Fourthly, I was able to accept an offer from friends to use their car if I needed to, and I have. Fifthly, I began to prioritise what journeys I actually needed to make and how environmentally I could make those.

Who would have thought that a car could give so many insights about letting go? That process led back to many unresolved issues in my life, and for that I am truly grateful. Letting go is the moment we allow ourselves to fragment, to surrender and be a hollow shell. It's often a time when we feel we have stepped into the void. When we are here, we are so close to where we need to be. But because of the emptiness we often struggle to get out of it or to cling on to what we think we have. It is, however, a time to rest, to let go of all worry and to surrender to the divine. The time to leave is when we are filled with light. It is then that we will truly have let go. Thank you, Rosie.

***** Exercises *****

How wide is your web of appreciation? Why not take twenty minutes or so and think of all the appliances, vehicles, people, countries, animals and aspects of the environment that might touch your life on a daily, weekly, monthly or yearly basis? Do you have a wish to give thanks for the offerings? How might you offer this? Could it be energetically, personally, politically, spiritually? Let your ideas creatively flow.

Trusting yourself – recall a time when you wished you had followed through with your first thoughts. If you were shown later that this would have worked for you better than the suggestion/advice taken, identify what the knock-on effects were for you and maybe others. Why not take this as sign that you are your own 'wise one'? When similar opportunities occur again, pledge yourself to going with yourself; after all, you now have evidence to back that up. It is time to trust your inner wisdom and to stand in your power.

What lessons were you born to learn? Look back over your life and examine what parental influences were around and how you might have chosen these folks for the lessons you needed to learn. Take personal responsibility; it is so empowering. Identify the pattern that those learnings have played out over the years. If you have children of your own, maybe you can see what their lessons may be and how you can lovingly support their path; after all, wouldn't it be great if they could get there quicker than you did?

Parenting and children – examine your values/beliefs. Are they truly yours? Ensure that you haven't inherited them from elsewhere and that they still serve you. Without blame/judgement, describe the qualities your parents had or you would have liked them to have. If you are a parent, describe the qualities you imagine your child/children would list as their experience of you. If you currently have a relationship with a child/children, however distant that might be, write a few sentences that describe how you would like that relationship to be. If that replicates the current situation, then great; if not, how might you bring that into fruition? Where are you witnessing situations either within your own family or externally where your beliefs and values are not being reflected? What action can you take?

What is your relationship with money? Often, we inherit our attitude towards money. Why not explore in a quiet space what its energy means to you. Try not to guide or censor your reaction. Allow it to take its own form. For some of us our lesson could be to hold onto it, for others to share it and there may be a multitude of other lessons, too. Ask what its lessons are for you in this lifetime. Remember that there is no right or wrong answer, just 'the answer'.

Working with grief – I would recommend starting your work by setting a clear intention and boundaries. This could be connected with the amount of time you wish to spend connecting with grief or the period of time within your life that you want to connect with; maybe keep it to family or relationship issues or go for whatever wants to present itself at that time. Ensure some uninterrupted time or, if you feel it would help, have a friend be with you to hold a space and witness your journey. Ask for your healing angels and guides to be with you and remember to be gentle with yourself. Invite your grief to surface. Were there any surprises? Why not keep a grief journal or a feeling journal and do this work with each of your feelings? Are there any celebrations?

Letting go – what aspects of life or traits might you benefit from if you were to let them go or reframe them? How have they been controlling you? What might you attract with the space you have created?

Heroin or a Cornish Pasty?

Self-sabotage

AT FIRST IT MAY SEEM RIDICULOUS TO SUGGEST THAT THESE words could be linked in the same breath, but for me that was exactly how they were experienced. Each has the potential to be a craving, a comfort, a blocker or even an addiction and definitely an act of self-sabotage.

My eldest son, now aged thirty, has been using drugs from the age of sixteen and has been a heroin addict on and off for most of that time. That obviously is not the sum of him, but it does have a great influence on the current part of his journey and mine.

I had travelled down to Exeter to pick him up upon his release from prison. He has been on a spiralling path of drugs, homelessness, shoplifting, prison, drugs, etc. This time, his release felt different. There was a glimmer of hope, as he had been offered a place on a rehab programme in his home town of Plymouth and had agreed to give it a go. The hope was dampened by the fact that, although he wanted to give up heroin, he had no intention of giving up cannabis. The rehab programme, however, was clear that there was to be no drugs of any description and no alcohol.

The plan was that he would leave prison on the Friday and arrive at the rehab centre on the Monday. In between, he was to keep clean, as he would be drug tested before entry. I had arrived hoping to persuade him to come with me and stay at a bed-and-breakfast place for the weekend, anywhere of his choice as long as it was not Plymouth. My brother had even given me some money to help cover the cost of it. Yet even as I drove down there I knew he wasn't going to go for it.

I want to admit that I've often fantasised about kidnapping him when he was released from prison and driving him up to a

Scottish island and living there with him, obviously with no means of escape, until we could wipe the slate clean and start again. There's a lot to be said for living on a Scottish isle. I spent a week myself on Erraid and it was one of the most moving weeks of my life, but that's another story.

Alternatively, I wanted to have enough money to afford an appointment for him with Deepak Chopra. When I was in Findhorn, I would work in the Cluny shop sometimes. I didn't do it for the money. In fact, I didn't know you got paid for doing it until after I accepted the job. Previously I had loved just going in there, not needing to purchase anything, just hanging around; 'deep in the presence of beauty' are the words of a song that comes to mind. One day, I was on duty, when I scanned the bookshelves for the book I needed to read that would help me right then. It was Deepak's book *Overcoming Addictions* that caught my eye. I asked the Universe which page I should open it at and started to read. It was obvious when I started reading that this was heaven-sent. Deepak was explaining by using a client as an example of a spiritual way to overcome addiction. The essence of what I remember its saying was that when he met up with this client he didn't ask her to speak about her addiction because no doubt this method had been used before and had been unsuccessful. He asked her to recall an activity which she had enjoyed in the past. She recalled that she used to love horse riding but it was not in her life now. She then agreed to undergo an Ayurvedic purification process called Panchakrama which detoxifies the mind, body and consciousness and rebalances one's beingness. In a short period of time his client felt reborn and after resting for a few days, she went horse riding. She loved the experience and it rekindled for her a positive memory of something that brought her joy: ecstasy. Interesting that the drug often used to find joy is called by the same name. However, as Deepak went on to prove with his client, this form of joy, which she found again with horse riding, did not have the same harmful side – the coming-down effect – as the heroin she had been taking for some years. After his client's horse riding event, Deepak asked her to explain to him in minute detail what it felt like to inject heroin into her body – asking her how it felt, what did the needle look like, feel like on her skin, etc.; exploring all her senses, such as what smells she remembered. What he was doing was asking her to be a witness to herself: being mindful, being present and in the now. As I was reading his words, all I kept thinking was that I hope one day my son will attract such an experienced guide/healer. Following on from her revelation about injecting heroin, Deepak asked his client to do the same exercise but relating to her experience of horse riding. This she was able to do much more easily, not just because it happened more recently but because of the detoxification process which had taken place. Deepak then asked his client which she would choose. She chose horse riding and released heroin. Please understand that this is just a short synopsis. It in no way implies that recovery from any addiction is easy. Recovery is for life and it involves a lot of work around self, groups and relationships.

I explained the technique to my son once when I was visiting him in prison, but I don't think it was the right time for him to hear it. It may have been due to the fact that he appeared to be stoned at the time. I'm dealing with my frustration at the difference between what our prison system says it wants to do and what it does or can do.

As it happened, my feeling was right and my son was not going to go along with my plan to go to a B&B. All he wanted to do was go back to Plymouth, see his friends and have some 'fun' before being locked up again. That was obviously what he felt about rehab at the time. Yet another place to be locked up in. I think he must be energetically linked to Plymouth in some way and it seems that nothing except visits to prison will keep him from it. Following my divorce from the children's father when my elder son was only four, I moved away from the area to Reading. When he was in his early teens, he begged me to let him go and live with his dad in Saltash, just over the bridge from Plymouth. His reason then was to live with a proper family that had a 'mum and dad', as I was still in a lone-parent situation. He came back to Reading aged sixteen when his father was at the end of his tether and had told him to leave.

Of course, I realise too that addicts will, until they are ready for a different lifestyle, return to the familiar. They need to know where their next fix is coming from. Where they can get it from what they perceive to be a reliable and safe source. Where people will let them stay in their homes for a while. Where they know shops they can steal from in order to feed their habit and to live. My own personal experience of engaging with the support agencies when I was unemployed in Swindon was horrific. I would consider myself an intellectual and assertive person, and even after six weeks of form-filling and turning up for appointments I still hadn't received any benefit. When I showed my documentation to the agencies, they said that I had been rejected due to the lack of certain paperwork that hadn't been previously presented. I pointed out that as I hadn't been in that position before, I had requested help at all stages from agency staff, especially as I was borderline dyslexic, and still I was told to start again. I then went on to appeal, and a few weeks later my appeal form was returned to me via the post office. 'Moved Away' was stamped across the letter. I just burst out laughing. Laughing at finally getting the hint from the Universe that this wasn't the right path for me. However, the insight I did get was how difficult it was for my son when leaving prison with very little money and being homeless. And, of course, for others in similar situations. How do we help them to cope or how do we support them in continuing their cycle?

I realise that in writing about this part of my life there is still some work to be done around guilt and reaching acceptance for my part. He is my son and he deserved the best. The way I choose to live with it is knowing that I did the best I could at the time. I'm a different person now and have many skills that I didn't have then. I also have a belief now that we choose our parents for the lessons we need to learn. Now that he is an adult, I feel my part is to honour his journey and hold nothing but love and respect for him as a soul. I don't condone the use of drugs or respect him for shoplifting and having an ASBO, but, as I've said before, that is not the sum of him. He is one of the most beautiful people I know. He has a heart of gold, is sociable and an excellent cook, has a sense of humour; despite all that he has been through, I can still see some self-worth, and he is still alive and relatively healthy considering his lifestyle. So you can imagine my feelings when I hadn't heard from him for a few months and did a search on the Internet. I searched for the local Plymouth paper and then put in '[his name+ASBO]', and lo and behold I got an article written the day after his twenty-seventh birthday. As you might imagine, it wasn't saying anything too complimentary, but I was mortally wounded to see the words 'and has been caged for six months'. Very emotive writing!

Back to picking my son up and receiving an emphatic, 'No.'

He went on to explain to me that he needed to connect with his drug counsellor when he got back to Plymouth and she was going to find him somewhere to stay until Monday morning, when he would be taken to rehab by an agency staff member.

'I need to do this for myself, Mum. If I can't do it over the weekend, then how can I do the programme?'

He knew I couldn't argue with that. We both knew, though, that he wasn't going to stay away from his old contacts and that he would take what he could get away with to allow him his place.

I met him on both the Saturday and the Sunday and it was like being on a rollercoaster ride for me. I would ache for the time we could spend together, just to be next to him, to touch him again, to hear him speak, to feel his love and to love him. Then there would be the throwing up and the 'buzzy energy' that surrounds those using drugs. I'm beginning to learn more about drugs and how they can affect you and those around you first hand. Part of me sometimes gets really cross that you can get drugs in prison. I can remember being horrified when I found there were 'drug-free' wings. Can you believe it? And even those are not totally drug-free. To me it was as if the prison service was accepting the use of drugs, even supporting it, and I wondered if a blind eye was turned as prisoners on drugs might help for a quieter life.

It has also got me wondering now if that is what we do as people: turn a blind eye to something that is happening in our lives, or to someone we love or work with. Not facing up to the truth of it because it makes us uncomfortable and we don't know how to rectify it. In a way, I was enacting that over the weekend. I didn't bring up the fact that I didn't believe he had stayed in the hotel room found for him. It was a lovely place and all his things were set out in the room, but it didn't feel lived in. I do believe he was genuinely grateful for the new clothes and the time we spent together, but I got the non-verbal messages very clearly when our time together was up. I didn't speak clearly to him about what I thought was happening or how I felt.

There would also be what felt like the 'normal' times when we could go for a drive or walk, have lunch, talk and go shopping. Obviously, with my son having an ASBO, we needed to travel to another town to get him some of the things he needed to take into rehab, such as clothes and toiletries. One thing about my son that hasn't changed is his need to be clean and tidy.

As we were heading out of the town, we stopped off at one of the large supermarkets to get him some food to last the weekend. After all, I didn't want him to have any excuse to go into a shop in Plymouth and therefore breach his ASBO. So there we were, choosing something from the salad bowl, when two men approached us. They looked at my son and asked what he was doing there. He explained he was shopping with me and I said that I knew he had an ASBO in Plymouth but thought it was OK for him to shop with me there. I then learnt that this supermarket chain has a policy that an ASBO in one town applies throughout the country. I know I'm going off the track a bit here, but how does anyone get out of this trap? All I feel I can do is send him the love and supportive energy he needs and hope that one day he will want to stop as much as he feels unable to now.

I want to take you back to after I arrived with my son in Plymouth. I had taken him to his drug counselling centre and he had asked me to wait in the car until he had found out what was happening next. It didn't take me long to work out what was happening. After he disappeared into the building, it was only a short time before he came out again with a couple of people and they huddled together behind some outbuilding. As I was deciding whether I should go over or not, they moved away and went back into the main building. About thirty minutes later, my son came out and said that he and his drug counsellor were going to be sorting out some accommodation and he would ring me later to let me know what was happening.

I decided to go into Plymouth town centre as a distraction. I don't know if I've ever felt so sick or so frightened in all my life. I had no idea what to do with myself. Robotically, I found a car park I knew and then headed into the town centre. I had a craving for a Cornish pasty and was heading towards one of the famous pasty shops when I stopped dead in my tracks. What the hell was I doing? Here I was a person who was wheat-free and dairy-free, heading off for an intake of something that was no good for me at all.

'Well, one won't hurt, will it?'

'Yes, it certainly will.'

The internal dialogue was so clear that I even wondered if I had said it out loud. Quickly, I looked around to see if anyone else had heard me. It was then it struck me that if I ate a pasty and gave into that craving now, how could I expect my son not to do that with heroin, which potentially had a larger hold over him than inappropriate comfort food had on me? Or had it? It made me start to wonder.

How many of us look for comfort externally, be it from food, sex, co-dependency relationships, smoking, watching the television, gambling, alcohol, shopping, cannabis, etc.? And how often then does it become more than a craving and turn into a fully fledged addiction? I looked back over my life at the addictions I thought I'd encountered. There had been times when I was addicted to drama, and boy, what a lot of energy that takes and what a lot of free time you have when you are no longer addicted to it. Along with the drama, I was addicted to being a victim. I also discovered that I'd been addicted to television as well. When I gave up my house at the start of this journey, I released all the televisions and didn't even keep one for my room at Ruskin College. When people asked me why not, I said I felt I would use it as a distraction to my studies. I was so right to do so. We did have a TV in the common room, but it was only near the end of my year that I started to use it. I say 'use' it because that was what I was doing. I had a gap in my life and I wanted it filled and I was using TV. It didn't benefit me; it just occupied me and distracted me. In Findhorn, there was little time or inclination for watching television, although there was a TV room in Cluny Hill College and again it was only near the end of my time there that I began to use it.

Please don't get me wrong; I'm not saying watching television is an addiction for everyone; but it definitely was for me. It took away a useful part of my life. When I returned from Croatia, I was living in a friend's house and she had a television. I was redecorating her house, and as the winter nights drew in I got into the habit of watching the box. One night I was lying on the sofa, watching a soap, when a thought came into my head: why are you watching other people's lives and not living your own? It felt such a truth to me that I instantly turned it off. The next night, when I was in the local Tesco's, I asked if they had any evening vacancies; surely it would be more beneficial working, connecting with people and earning some money than watching the television. I told a friend this, and by the next day I'd got the names of two people who she thought might have part-time jobs for me. I got them both, plus another job for when I'd completed my friend's house, and this one offered me accommodation in exchange for the hours I worked.

When I moved into the studio flat, there was no television; I was offered about four and refused them all. It was amazing how after only a few months of watching it again I was looking for it in the evenings and at weekends. It reminded me of withdrawal symptoms that those who misuse drugs and alcohol might go through. Not that I'm comparing the intensity, but for me it was my hell for about two weeks, until I found other things to do. Now, when I go into a house where I'm living, I have a mantra: I use the television wisely and respect the valuable things it can offer me.

I've also used food and drink for comfort, and for me they have both been bordering on addiction and have definitely been self-sabotaging agents. So it is no wonder that now I drink mostly water and never drink alcohol. I'm also vegan, eating organic food wherever possible, and have a wheat-free diet. My body is so much healthier, my skin is clearer and I have more energy. Oh, yes, I've cut down on the sugar content, too, although I do enjoy treats once in a while.

So you see that if I hadn't put heroin and a Cornish pasty together in one thought I might not have discovered the number of addictions I actually had myself. I thought the best way I could help my son was to clean up my own habits.

I subsequently engaged on a twelve-step programme for family members of addicts. I wanted to ensure that I was not 'enabling' my son to stay in the loop. It is with love and dedication that I dedicate the following poem to my son and all sons and mothers.

My Beautiful Boy

When will you remember, is my prayer,
that you are loveable and others care?
What happens to you in life does matter
You're not a throw away like a paper platter.

You are my son who I love so much
And my heart is breaking without your touch.
Your smile, your eyes, your sense of fun
Oh when, I wonder, did this all go wrong?

We can go into the childhood years
feeling the pain and releasing the tears.
We can talk through the first fix and the ones after that
Of children's home, prison, heroin and crack.

I can't imagine what life is like for you
With never a job, no career to pursue.
No building yet to call your home.
No people around, no one to phone.

No one to turn to for respect and advice,
unless you count mates who come at a price,
who expect you to pay for the drugs with your life,
which is passing each day without children or wife.

No dream to fulfil save to find the next fix,
will you sleep in a bed or be found in a ditch?
Will I dance with you dressed in our Sunday best
or will I carry your coffin and lay you to rest?

Will you keep the promises made to your son
or will he only know of you when you have gone
When he visits your grave feeling lost and sad
For being robbed of spending time with his dad?

No one can give you back those years.
You were robbed for sure, but there's no time for tears.
Go for the jugular with determination and guts
And reach inside to a place you can trust.

That will remind you of the person you were born to be
And remember why you chose to be a son to me.
You have lots to give and more to receive,
But you need to begin NOW or there'll be no reprieve.

Your body, no longer vibrant, shows signs of decay.
I remember the boy who would seek me out to play.
Beneath the mist and cloudy shape, I see
The spark of light which shows me all you can be.

***** Exercises *****

Do you have some habits that could be a form of addiction? The invitation is to spend a bit of time looking at how they are affecting you and those around you. What would it be like to give them up? What might you do with the amount of energy, time or money you previously spent on them? Do you think there is a pattern of people who are currently around you or whom you draw to you where this has or is being played out? How might some healing for all be carried out?

The Joys of Getting a Parking Ticket

Always Looking for the Lessons

I THINK THE FIRST THOUGHT I HAVE WHEN I SPEAK OR WRITE about anything like the joys of getting a parking ticket is people responding with, 'Oh, people like you just make me sick, always seeing the positive side of things,' or 'Here comes Jacqueline again with her positive door-opening attitude.'

Both of these were actually said to me with a negative slant attached to them. In the past, I used to cringe and shrink away when I heard these responses, but I don't apologise for it any more. It's who I am, it's the way I choose to see life, and I thank God that it works that way for me. I also honour the fact that not everyone has to think that way and from my perspective it's OK for people to have an alternative view. Regardless of how you currently choose to see the world, I'd love to tell you the story, so here's hoping that you can see what I got out of it.

I was living in central Reading at the time and had been awarded a parking permit for my car, but when I sold her the permit could not be used for another car without completing the relevant paperwork. I was lucky enough to have some friends who were willing to lend me their car when I needed it, and it is to one such occasion that this story relates. I'd borrowed it to take a run down to Plymouth to spend some time with my grandson, who was celebrating his fifth birthday. The trip went well and I was keeping the car in Reading with me for a few more days before it was time to return it to my friends in Didcot. I hadn't had a chance to make a permit transfer, as I was awaiting some documents, so my options were either to park it on a piece of waste ground about four minutes' walk away or to put my temporary day pass on it when I was parking it in the street.

On the day in question, I was working for Mencap in Henley,

and as I was driving over I made my usual request to the universe, 'It would be great to have a parking space right outside the house, please.' Yet for whatever reason – maybe my energy was low – I had this lack of belief about the request. It might not have been high up in my awareness, but I could feel it lurking there somewhere. It was like some self-doubt working very subtly in my lower consciousness. As I approached the street I would be working in, I saw a parking space at least a dozen houses up from the actual house where I would have liked a space and I can remember thinking that this would be as near as I could get. Why did I doubt I could get nearer? Why did I limit myself? So I parked there, got my stuff out of the car and started walking down to my place of work. As I got nearer to the house, I saw with amazement that there was a space, big enough for about two cars with room to spare, directly outside the house.

I asked myself what this meant. For me, it was about not trusting myself in being able to ask for and receive what I needed. I guess that might be true for a lot of us. I know that asking people for what I needed or not asking them has created a few dramas in my life. I can remember a period in my life when I would be fearful about asking people to babysit for me because I would feel rejected if someone said no or blame them for not supporting me in attempting to get a little bit of fun into my life. Thankfully, that part of me is healed and I can ask freely for what I want because I've learnt not to attach any expectation to my request. What has also transpired is that sometimes I don't even have to ask and yet it still arrives. I guess it's the law of attraction working on a subtle level. However, the request for the car parking space was tinged with something I hadn't witnessed in myself for a while. I had asked for the same thing many times before and it was usually provided. It wasn't about attaching an expectation, because I could accept whatever happened. I believe it was because I had a niggling feeling there was a lesson here and I didn't want to lose the opportunity to gain from it.

It was only later in the evening, when the clients were going to bed and I was about to leave, that the answer came to me. Why did I not trust in myself and my Source? I don't know about you, but I've had lots of stuff to work with and process in my life, and I got to the stage where I felt I'd dealt with all I knew about. So I couldn't understand when out of the blue it would pop up again. When this happens now, I believe it is because it's in my subconscious, maybe something from when I was a child, something I've blocked out, or even from another lifetime. So when I ask for healing now I ask that it takes place on all levels in all directions of time.

So there I was at around 11 p.m., having finished my shift and driving home. I was feeling pleased about having a great shift and looking forward to getting into bed. When I got back to Reading, I was tired and it was raining, so instead of parking the car on the wasteland I parked it outside my house and asked the angels to protect it from the traffic wardens for me. I was thinking that this would be my chance to show how much I was prepared to trust. However, when I look back on it, I was also saying, 'Well, God, I trust you; prove to me that my trust is returned.'

I went straight to sleep that night thinking that all was very, very well.

I awoke in the morning with this huge sense of love filling every part of my body. It felt as if I were in love. I couldn't believe the intensity of it. I was grateful for the memory. It was as if I were in love with myself and my life and it made my heart sing. I felt as passionate about myself as I had in the past about another. I felt so close and intimate with myself and my Source. After doing some journaling, I got up and put on my clothes so that I could move the car before I pushed my luck with the traffic wardens. As I went out of the door, I got this funny feeling in my stomach and my eyes caught sight of a bright yellow plastic packet fixed to the windscreen.

So what was this all about, I was thinking. Here I am, filled with love, and I'm faced with this! I have choices, I told myself, reminded of the work of Ekhart Tolle and his book, *The Power of Now*. My choice was to refuse to go into a drama about this or to step out from the state of love that filled me. It was then that my mind started to filter what had happened. Firstly, I hadn't trusted I was going to get a parking space and was shown that, had I believed, I would have got one. Secondly, when I believed my car would be protected it was proved that it wasn't. What was going on? I knew it wasn't about punishment, because I believe God doesn't want me to suffer; he/she only wants me to learn. I took the question inside and was quiet for a few minutes when I got the answer. God was there all along on both occasions, like he/she always is. Guiding me, teaching me, holding a space for me. Not judging or blaming, just waiting for me to ask what the lesson was and then lovingly showing me in such a way that I could learn for myself. The bit of me that had been playing out the night before was the part of me that lacked self-belief, while the bit of me that was alive today was the part of me that wanted justice and fairness.

I was asked two questions: 'Would you want to work with a God who bent the law?' which was closely followed by 'Why didn't you use the resources you have been given?'

There was nothing more that needed to be said. Of course, my answer to the first question was a strong 'no'. I know I ask the angels to protect my car when I park it and when I drive in it, but what I had been asking for the night before was not the same. I had been asking for something to be proven to me by bending the law. Of course, I didn't realise that was what I was asking for at the time, but now that it was clear to me, I was glad to have received the ticket. Had that not been the case, I would have gone down a false path. The question about using the resources was really helpful, too, as I did think about putting a day permit on my car, but I knew I didn't have very many, so I didn't want to use one unnecessarily and then run out. I realised that it was also a test, and that is very different from trust. Tests don't come from a place of love; they come from fear. I think the lesson about trusting that there will always be enough for what I need is a common one and has been experienced by others I interact with.

I noticed this lack of abundance alive in me again just before I took myself down to Ashbury to write this book, the book I had been promising myself I would write for the last three years. I was being offered everything I asked for. I'd decided that this was it; if I didn't write this book now, I was never going to do it. I was also fed up of carrying it around with me. It was like a weight on my back and I wanted to travel more lightly. I'd been doing some visualisation work since giving notice on my job and the accommodation I received in exchange. The house I kept seeing, although not identical from the outside, did in fact have everything in the same place. It was as if I'd remotely viewed it. Even down to an organic plot of land to grow some vegetables on. I had also visualised a separate building in the grounds, which I could offer to my younger son and his partner at the time. I had thought that this was a converted stable, and there were some horses in the field, which would please my son's partner. Although this outbuilding was not included at the house at Ashbury, my son and his partner moved into their first house the weekend I moved and I'm in horse riding and racing country. The other thing I visualised was that I owned it. I suppose that was all about a need for security, as I was down to the last £1,500 of my savings.

I had also asked for a three-month gap of time for me to concentrate on my writing. The contract offered with the house at Ashbury was for six months, and with the savings I had left I could only afford three, maybe four, months. I still went for a visit, and you can imagine my surprise when I realised the similarities to my visualisation, except, of course, the part about me being the owner. Almost everything else was what I had previously seen. I'm grateful to the owners of the property, who offered to reduce the tenancy agreement to three months, and to a friend who offered to sponsor me for two further months. I was giving up two jobs to go there and I wasn't able to guarantee what work I would attract to sustain myself; this would be another lesson of concentration on abundance, not lack. Both the instance with the day parking ticket and my savings were examples to me of letting things flow. Letting them work for me, rather than holding on to them and blocking myself. As I've said before, thoughts are great manifestors – choose the right ones. The well-known saying 'be careful what you wish for, because you might get it', I am taught, goes deeper than the surface level of thinking. Watch out for it.

Going back to the parking ticket, there was a further lesson to come my way on this one. As I went to write my cheque, it occurred to me that I should write it with love, the state I had been given that morning. I wanted it to be a willing act. When I moved back to Reading, I had decided that I wasn't going to do anything that didn't bring me joy. I had been given an opportunity to learn and grow, and I thought of the many workshops and courses I'd been on and how happy I'd been to hand over the money for those. This seemed exactly the same for me. After all, as an environmentalist, I did understand what the local authority was trying to do regarding cars in the town centre. Sometimes, if I only concentrate on my needs and wants, I can lose sight of the bigger picture. I'm definitely not suggesting we give up on our own needs, but that we take an opportunity to look at something with a wider perspective, to achieve a balance, something that works for the good of all.

This was a gentle nudge for me and I learnt a lot by looking for the positive aspect rather than the negative. The alternative would have been to give up on God, blame the traffic warden, the local authority and then myself for having to pay out thirty pounds. I choose to believe it was money well spent. With regard to the savings, this was to come to me again right at the end of writing this book. Keeping the last few pounds in my bank account and blocking me from doing things that needed to be done was not helping. So I released the money and I feel I have learnt the lesson now.

***** Exercises *****

Do you have a positive outlook on life? Is your glass half-full or half-empty? Is the world a wretched place to live in or is it a beautiful place where sometimes 'negative' stuff happens? Do you believe that people are only there to achieve things for themselves? Do you believe in lack or abundance?

Are you witnessing a lack of faith in something currently? Are you about to give up five minutes before a miracle might happen? Try to remember a time when everything in your life was flowing and it seemed that miracles were happening every moment. What would it feel like to capture that feeling again now? Now visualise your current issue and see its solution unfold. Know that it is safely in God's hands and already healed. The invitation is to forget about it now, as worry and negative thoughts only hinder the resolution.

Do you remember a recent or past incident that you considered a negative experience? Was there a lesson there and were you able to embrace it lovingly? If not, how would it feel if you were to fill yourself with love and go back to visualise how it might now be reflected back to you?

What is your current experience with regard to asking and receiving? Think about some of the things you have asked for. Have you attached an expectation to the request? How did you feel when you did or didn't get the response you were expecting? Do you think the person you were requesting from felt the expectation attached to it? How do you think they may have felt? Could it have affected the outcome? How would it feel to ask and be able to say 'thank you' whether it was a yes or a no? When you received something recently, did it have an expectation attached to it? Was it placed there by the giver or yourself?

Have you been self-limiting with yourself, your thoughts, your dreams? Why not play with the idea that all the things you desire are possible? Release any limits relating to money, physical energy, other people, geography, time, other commitments, qualifications. Why not use visualisation as a tool for manifesting your fullness? Have you ever stopped yourself going for a job or course because you didn't have the qualifications? Have you thought that you couldn't be somebody's parent/partner/lover because you weren't good enough, thin enough or beautiful enough? Find some quiet time for yourself and visualise what it would be like to be as powerful as you could be with your thoughts and dreams, allowing your higher self to play the game

How would you feel if you did only things that brought you joy? Would you feel guilty, selfish, self-centred or uncaring? Would it be possible for you to think that you could be living your purpose? Doing the things you were meant to do? Being your true self? Could you be connected to your Source and working from that place?

Finding Your True North

The Person You Were Born To Be

WHILE I HAVE BEEN GROUNDING MY EXPERIENCES IN THE telling of this story, there has come for me an even greater opportunity for learning and transformation. As for many people, it has always been a very natural thing for me to share what I have. Therefore it follows that I share my recent experiences in the hope that they may be of use to another. These experiences have lifted me in so many ways that it would feel a crime to keep the information to myself. Even if the only person it helped was me, its writing will have been worthwhile. They say everyone has a book in them. Funnily enough, as I'm writing this, my first book, I am enjoying playing with the idea that it may be the first of many. Maybe I have found a new passion?

I have always loved being a homemaker and craved to be part of a vibrant, loving family. Equally, I have always been enthusiastic about sustainability and more recently about abundance, whether it be in an intimate loving relationship, health, money, our planet or oneness. On reviewing my life, I can see that I have often been close to my purpose, my given pathway, but have sometimes veered a little off course. Discovering my own inner compass – my voice within, my connection with Source – has enabled me to know where my true north is.

As a young teenager, I loved to write and paint. I would often spend time on my own, inventing stories or finding bits of discarded furniture or stones that I could paint flowers on. I even asked for oil paints one year for Christmas. Yet I had not, it seemed, found a way to convey what I was trying to express so that another could see its beauty. Communication and creativity were obviously two of the things I had agreed to come here to work with.

It appears that I also came with an abundance of tenacity, which has at times been a double-edged sword. Things often are, aren't they? People often admire the drive, determination, steadfastness, but evaluate it differently when they see it as stubbornness and obstinacy. Yet all of those make up the whole. I suppose it will depend on which part of us is being triggered. In my early years, I was determined not to let others see my feelings or my tears. In later years, it became obvious that I was holding onto a fair amount of pain and I subsequently vowed to release it. I have discovered that when I express an invitation such as this to the Universe, I am usually heard and responded to. Issues, triggers, challenges or conflict, both inner and outer, will arise and offer me the opportunity to process, release, heal and transform. I choose to be present with what comes up for me now and work through it as it arises. Not to divert my attention away from it with food, television, ringing a friend, going shopping or mowing the lawn. I understand now that it is useful for me to accept, that part of my healing will come through the natural flow of my tears. In the past, I would have stubbornly held onto them. Pushed them down, along with my anger, and been determined to hold them deep inside me. I have chosen to reframe how I look at my feelings and tears. They are no longer a weakness. My vulnerability is my strength and I see my tears as jewels, pearls of wisdom. Like an oyster, my shell has been cracked open. With the fleshy me exposed, I am now able to see the beautiful pearl which was previously kept from view. Now, whenever possible, I allow my tears to flow.

At the commencement of this journey, I was receiving some counselling and the subject of tears came into the conversation. It was noticed that I would always try to hold them back. I was asked how many tears I had to cry, and as a forty-nine-year-old woman I said six weeks' worth. That was six weeks non-stop, 24/7. It came to me on a silent meditative walk one day how best I might work with this information. I was by the river in a small village on the outskirts of Oxford when I came across a lock and an insight just struck me. This was how it was best for me to process. The river leading up to the lock was my past, and the water in the lock represented the 'bite-size pieces' that I could deal with at any one moment in time. Once processed, tears would be released as symbolised by the weir and the water flowing downstream represented my future. It felt so beautiful to see it in that way. It definitely wasn't in my consciousness to look for a remedy. Since my awakening, things were gently coming to me, and I was and still am constantly very grateful.

Now, when I think of myself as a hurt little girl, I am filled with an overwhelming feeling of love for her. The way she hung on in there, knowing that there was injustice but she was just 'too little' to be heard. I always feel blessed when I have the opportunity to work with children and parents either individually or together. I feel both have a right to a rich, fulfilling experience and am happy to be part of that unfolding. Often I found that if the adult has unhealed childhood issues they have a 'double whammy'. They discover that they need to work with their children and their own inner child at the same time. If, like me, the self-healing comes after the children have reached maturity, then the 'double whammy' can feel equally painful. Once I'd reaccessed my childhood pains, I was at first horrified by the potential pain I may have subsequently caused to my children. However, I now review my life with the concepts of personal responsibility, forgiveness and acceptance. I am able to realise and accept that I have done the best job I can with the resources I had at the time. This has enabled me to look back at my childhood and trust that the same must stand for those around me while I was growing up. I believe that we are all children of the Universe and therefore we deserve the best experiences. I appreciate being able to work with people who want to achieve that. Bringing dreams to reality is an absolute joy for me. These realisations are all part of my connecting to my true north and working with others who want to do the same. It is the North Star that will guide us home.

When I look back, I can see where these dreams have been bubbling away and how all my experiences have brought me to where I was at the time of writing this book: living in a shared, holistic house and helping to create a vibrant, loving 'family'; working with people individually and in groups; creatively expressing myself through my writing and connecting with children or the child within. It is from this place that we truly heal.

I have always felt a strong connection with children and enjoyed their being part of my life. As a young wife, I hoped that I would have at least six children of my own. Biologically, I am a mother of two sons and a miscarried daughter. I have through my life felt like a Pied Piper at times, as many children have been attracted to me. When my own children were young, our home would be filled with their friends and children met through my connections with Gingerbread, a single-parent family support group. I have always been happy to connect with them. Even those described as the naughtiest or most difficult to handle were usually willing to share their beauty with me. On days out or holidays, I would experience such wonderful conversations with children and would feel richer for the connections. It is probably because of my own childhood experiences and that of parenting my children that I am now particularly drawn towards working with the Indigo and Crystal children. I believe that they are a blessing to us at this moment in our planet's history. I feel that it can't always be easy for them to live to their fullest potential if the adults, siblings and peer groups connected with them are unaware of their life's purpose. Often over the last couple of years I have noticed that some babies and young children have an unspoken connection with me. Their gaze has been sustained longer than I've noticed with other children. It feels as if there is another form of communication going on. I love to take the opportunity to smile back at them, to let them know that with my current awareness I appreciate, understand and am grateful for their being here. Having shared this experience, I have found that other adults are aware that they have this connection, too. I'm remembering the occasion on which I went to a World Angel Day Event hosted by Diana Cooper and Doreen Virtue. Many things inspired me that day and indeed changed my life. It was the day I chose to release meat and alcohol from my diet. That was the easy part. The hardest bit was when the auditorium was addressed and an invitation put out for those who were drawn to work with children to stand up. How I wanted to be one of those who stood up. I felt myself rising, but my humanness was pushing me back onto the chair. Why? I didn't feel I was good enough. I chose to see my life's experiences as a detriment to my suitability for that work, rather than a gift. I'm thankful to have turned that thought around.

For most of my life, I resolved to challenge maltreatment and injustice, even though as a child I was often shut down. Being shut down so young, for something I felt inside was so right, led me to experience difficulties in expressing my emotions. This over the years caused me to become hardened. I opted for that, as my survival technique. I chose early to play the roles of the victim, the rebel, even the self-saboteur. I decided I didn't have any choice – this was my lot. When I look back, I can see that in a funny way I learnt acceptance and surrender very early on. However, I now feel that I was a bit off-course with their application. It's no wonder, therefore, that those two attributes were the most difficult for me to reframe. For me, that's an excellent example of not denying or judging any of our traits. I try not to think of things as good or bad, right or wrong, or even one end of the spectrum or another. Reframing the aspects of a victim helped me see that the qualities of an aggressor can also be appraised differently; being focused, getting the job done and standing in your power are positive traits. I've chosen not to deny any of my past but instead look back to see where it has brought me closest to my true path, rather than focusing on being miles off course and assuming it was my lot. From a place of personal responsibility, I chose to take nearly fifty years before I started to want to heal, to find my true north. No two of us are the same. Some can heal in a moment; for others it could take a lifetime. My belief is that we are here to discover who we were born to be and what our purpose and mission is. It is from a place of healing that mine is unfolding. Whether it is in our childhood or in our last moments, most of us will find that we were never too far adrift from our true self.

My prayer is that this book aids the discovery of your true north at a time that serves your journey to its highest good. I believe that none of us can heal another but that our purpose is to heal ourselves and in so doing we will aid either directly or indirectly the healing of many. My understanding is that we don't have to do it alone. We can seek and offer support and enjoy the company of fellow travellers. There are many of us taking this journey at this particular moment – more than previously. We can work in isolation or we can collaborate. For me, there have been times when each of these has served me best. I believe it is my responsibility to look and reach inward first for any healing, guidance or answers I need. When I perceive that the answers are not coming, I use the world and my relationships as mirrors for insights and potential setbacks. Collaborative working has also been very constructive for me and I am honoured when individuals agree, at whatever level, to connect with me for mutually beneficial healing. I suppose that is a reason why I enjoy working with couples, groups, families or organisations to arrive at a place of richness, oneness through openness, sharing and mediation. I enjoy helping myself and others find the place where our oneness meets. Where we are all 'being at one' with our true self and connecting to each other from our place of Source. For this to work well, individuals often need to offer up their vulnerability, and this takes strength, courage and trust. This is often a place where we are closest to Source and where we can close down or remain closed depending on our previous experiences. My desire in these instances is to hold a space for that re-opening. To respect what I am witnessing in myself or another and to see where I can help build a bridge. To honour that desire, that dream of connection, of oneness, and to enable it to become a reality.

By sharing our stories, our gifts and talents, we are developing the blueprint that will take us all home: where we are at one with ourselves and the people around us, where we accept abundance as the norm and fear is no longer part of our composition. Where peacefulness, joy and gratitude are with us from the moment we wake until our head touches the pillow. Where we are continually accepted for who we truly are – a soul whose beauty shines forth and reflects back the beauty of another. For me, it is no longer a dream, a whimsical idea; for me, it is becoming a reality. I suppose that's why I now enjoy working as a Spiritual Dreambuilder. It was from a place of reconnection with my soul and Source, a place where I connected with my spirituality, that my ideas started to become a way of life for me. I no longer think about what I'd like to be. I've become it. There were stepping stones; first I needed to find my compass, then my true north and finally my destination. I accept that once I get there a new journey and destination will open up for me. So I am learning to embrace the mystery tour I'm on, as it leads me to sites and experiences that I would never have known existed. I sometimes imagine that there are angels around me, holding a large clipboard or a rainbow-coloured umbrella saying 'This way for the mystery tour. Follow me.' Guess what? I've even discovered that some other people think that happens, too.

Often in life I have felt alone, a stranger among my family. Not picked or part of the group. Oh, I did so want to be picked, a trait which was to play out in my life many times before I became aware of it. I also chose at an early age to frame my life based on what I didn't want, unaware that the Universe doesn't hear the word 'not'. I didn't want to be abused, selfish, limited in the beliefs of myself or the world around me. I didn't want to be a victim, a single parent, a matriarch or to live within the boundaries of fear. I became each and every one of them.

When I look back, I can see that there have always been signposts that could have got me back on course. When I was born, I was given free will, and I can see what routes I chose and where I expressed it. After my experience with forgiveness, I realise that it no longer serves me to look back and blame or judge another or myself for what happened. What serves me best is taking responsibility for my life, all of it, and living in the moment. A lot more being than doing.

The discovery of my inner compass, my inner voice, my connection with Source has been truly life-changing for me. I wasn't knowingly looking for it. In fact, for many years I would have ridiculed any concept of the divine or spirituality in general, especially the notion of an inner voice or guidance. I would have scorned the idea of miracles, psychic abilities, healing, communing with animals and nature. I would have mocked the idea of having a spiritual practice. I would have scoffed at the thought that any of these could be part of my life. When they started to come, my second reaction was to resist and deny them, opposing them in whatever way I could. I can remember that before I went to Findhorn a friend lent me a book by Eileen Caddy, one of its founders. I had never heard of her before. Even before looking at the book, I held a huge opposition to knowing what she had to say. As soon as I started to read, I felt that my intuition was right: she was definitely a lady to avoid. It was 'God' this and 'God' that. Where did she think she was coming from? Apparently, God was supposed to be talking to her and giving her guidance.

Well, she certainly has lost the plot, I thought. Best stay away from the likes of her. Don't want to be tainted with the same brush or my family will certainly disown me.

It wasn't just that. Her partner, who later became her husband, Peter Caddy, also carried out the guidance she received. The strange thing is that, even though at the time I was opposing what I was reading in Eileen's book, I was still planning my trip to Findhorn a few months hence. In fact, my place on Experience Week had already been booked. There was no logic, I know. All I can now do on reflection is witness it and have a bit of a chuckle to myself. I put Eileen's book down for a few weeks and then for some reason I picked it up again, but this time I started to read the final pages. It was amazing. I could totally connect with everything she was saying. A shift had come about because in the later pages the word 'God' barely appeared. Part of my resistance obviously was to the word 'God', but it was also to the idea that it was possible for communication to exist with God. I found the strength of my resistance to this woman, whom I had never met before, very strange. I was also prejudiced at the time because I was judging that it must be a huge ego that would believe itself able to receive guidance from God. I held memories from this lifetime when I perceived that people who were doing something in 'God's' name were often coming from a 'power-over' base. I was tarring her with the same brush.

Experience Week and subsequent programmes I attended at Findhorn allowed me to explore the wonderment and the magic of the place. I noticed that I was always keen to avoid Eileen. Eventually, though, I was destined to meet her. It was during the three-month Foundation Programme I attended, nine months after my first visit, when I noticed that as a group we were scheduled to meet her one morning. Again I could feel my hackles rising and the resistance gaining strength. My reasoning told me that there was nothing between the two of us in this lifetime that would explain my reaction. I had not met her and did not even know enough about her to form an opinion. This was something greater than that, but I still couldn't explain what was playing out.

OK, I said to myself. Let's see this 'Miracle Woman' at work, then.

Many of the people in my group were keen to meet her, held her in high regard and even spoke of her reverently. Not me, though. When she came into the Park Sanctuary to meet us, I knew that if the opportunity presented itself I would speak my mind to her. We shared a meditation together and then she spoke to us about her life at Findhorn. There was also time for a question and answer session. In truth, I found her on one level to be very amenable, but still rumbling around was this 'Who do you think you are to sit there saying you can receive communication from God?' feeling going on inside me. My turn presented itself, and I think I said something along the lines of, 'I don't believe you have to sit still and be silent to connect with God. I think he can connect with us through our dance or our singing.'

I guess you will have noticed that there had been a shift in my acceptance: firstly that there was a God, and secondly that there was the ability to communicate. I could no longer deny that. I was experiencing it and had done so from the fifth day of my very first visit to Findhorn. But I had pushed it down. I had refused to accept it for myself.

I can't remember her exact reply, but what I felt from her answer was an inner knowing. It was at odds to my mental and emotional state. At a deeper level, I knew it was the truth. It was fear that was preventing the connection. The acceptance of that truth was keeping me from seeing her light. It was some time later before I realised that she was sitting there as a mirror. It was an image of me that I saw reflected back. It was scary. It's amazing how much easier it has been for me to see the negative traits reflected back to me, the opportunities to improve, to be better, to heal. It was a while before I understood that healing was also required around acceptance of who I truly was. A wise elder woman, knowing and accepting her true self, communing with Spirit, walking her talk, evolving and sharing her stories.

A couple of years later, while surfing the internet, I came across a quote by Arthur Schopenhauer (1788–1860), a German philosopher. It spoke volumes to me and I'd love to share it with you. 'Every truth passes through three stages before it is recognised. In the first, it is ridiculed. In the second, it is opposed. In the third it is regarded as self-evident.' All three of those stages had played out for me with this scenario. I have a feeling that maybe Eileen and I have had some past-life exchanges and that may have been what I was reacting to.

Since knowing that, I have identified two other women who have had similar experiences with me. We had vowed all those lifetimes ago not to gather together again. The fear of the persecution was so strong and the pain of what unity might bring to a 'fellow sister' was too much to bear. Like Peter and his denial of Christ, here I was again denying another.

In life these days, I mostly feel that I know who I truly am at any given moment. With the help of my inner compass, I am able to identify when I'm off course, what is being triggered and which out of my physical, emotional or mental body has been activated. It is from this place I can plot my new route. It is at this stage that my free will kicks in and I can decide to stay off-course or to journey back to my true north.

With the reawkening of my spirituality and my reconnection with Source, my life is certainly more joyous. I feel happier and healthier than I have ever before in my life. There seems to be greater potential for myself and those around me, including the beautiful planet that we live upon. I have witnessed the power of fear on a personal and global level, and for me it seems it always projects itself from a controlling base and a 'power-over' desire. I now choose acceptance and surrender any day. I hold an acceptance that there is a level where we are all one. Whatever is mirrored back to me is a reflection of me, whether it is something that might have pleased or displeased me in the past. Acceptance of who I am and how I am performing is reflected by my inner compass. I no longer need to look outwardly for approval, praise, permission or for my needs to be met. I AM. This for me means that I am my own 'soulmate'. I am the mother, father, sister, brother, lover, mentor. That doesn't mean that I don't enjoy the company of other souls or indeed want to work with them, live with them and be in relationships with them. It does mean that I am complete, in my wholeness, in the wholeness. No longer is there the constant conflict between my shadow and light side, my feminine and masculine energies, my ying and yang, God and Gaia, scientific and esoteric or my inner child and my adult/parent. For me this brings harmony and allows my energy to be redirected to inner and outer growth. It is from this place that I can choose to surrender and the lines from one of the poems shared with you before come to mind: *it has brought me to a beautiful place where all in my heart seems right. I choose to give myself complete; no longer afraid, I don't fight.* It is from here that I am willing to surrender to the divine all that I am. I am willing to be healed and to serve the greatest good. It is from here that I have faith that my gifts and talents will be used for the whole and that I will receive all that I need to carry out this work. From here, I have learnt to take things lightly, to be the lighter side of spirituality, to connect with my Archangel of Fun and with my laughter chakra. It is from here that my compass will guide me home.

> Too often we decide to follow a path that is not really our own, one that others have set for us. We forget that whichever way we go, the price is the same: in both cases we will pass through both difficult and happy moments. But when we are living our dreams the difficulties we encounter make sense.
>
> Paulo Coelho, *The Alchemist*

***** Exercises *****

Journaling – before writing this book I kept journals for about three years, sometimes as a day-to-day journal and on other occasions when I was working on a particular aspect of myself such as grief, intuition, purpose. Writing your thoughts and feelings can be very powerful. I would invite you to keep a journal for a month about whatever topic comes to you first. You may find you want to continue it for a lot longer.

What do you feel passionate about? Take ten minutes to write a list and see what comes through for you. When you look at the list, can you see a pattern? Are your passions trying to take you in a certain direction? Is one of them your true north, the one you are truly connected to? How might that be connected to your purpose/mission?

The Universe and the word 'not' – how often do you use the word 'not' in relation to what you don't want to happen? Do you have examples in your life where what you have not wanted has happened? How can you rephrase your 'not' requests to the Universe so they are received as positives? Monitor the changes.

Roles/archetypes we play – looking back on your life, can you identify what roles/archetypes you may have been playing out? Do they still serve you? Can you identify their traits? How might you reframe them to work with you in connecting with your true self?

Which roles, if any, did you use as survival techniques? How would it feel to move through and beyond survival? What would you need to let go of? What would you want to bring forward?

Individual Processing – what works best for you when you want to connect with and process a learning? Do you need quiet time?

Would it help to write it down? Why not write a letter to someone you have an issue without sending it? A few weeks later, write the letter you would wish to receive back. How do you feel about that issue now? Alternatively, why not take a walk in nature and have a conversation with the fairies? Tell them exactly how you feel about an issue. As you carry on walking, look to see what gets reflected back to you. Know that it is OK to cry or to be angry. Own it, work with it appropriately and be compassionate with yourself about how you feel.

Communication – what works well for you with regards to communication? What are your gifts? Are there any lessons for you to learn around that? What would it be like for you to have a conversation with God or Source? What might be said back to you?

Acceptance – which aspects of your life would benefit from acceptance? What might you need to own/take responsibility for? What might you need to release?

How near do you feel that you are to your right path? Who or what might have influenced the course you are taking? Identify the challenges. Examine which ones make sense and which don't. What steps might you need to take to place you back on course?

Walking My Talk

Being and Celebrating My True Self

CONGRUENCE HAS ALWAYS BEEN SOMETHING THAT HAS been close to my heart. As a child, I didn't always witness it around me, and I guess when I see it lacking now it gives me the opportunity to look inside and search my hidden corners. I am grateful to discover that I usually find something I'm willing to become more congruent with. For me, it is the same as 'walking the talk'. The people who inspire me most are those within whom I witness that happening. That doesn't mean that they need to be the most enlightened beings on the planet; often, it seems that children can be my greatest teachers. What it means is that they are doing the very best they can to connect with their true self and Source and to illustrate that through generously sharing their gifts and talents.

Learning to walk a spiritual path is one thing, walking it another. After three years of taking time out to discover mine, I have had the opportunity to begin to know my true self. I have become acquainted and formed an intimate relationship with what I call Source. Now I feel it is time for me to put that learning into practice; it's time to walk my talk, to allow my dreams to become a reality.

Don't think for one moment that I am doing this without fear. It is around. What I have done, though, is form a new relationship with it. When I feel its presence, I'm reminded of the respect that I have for myself, the subject matter and the people who may be touched by what I do. My fear, which often manifests as resistance, reminds me that I'm on the right track. Fear no longer stops me writing; what it does is connect me to the parts of me that may feel unworthy, not good enough, that says:

'What's so special about what you have to say?'

'You're only saying what others have said.'

'What if you let Source down?'

So my fear plays against my inner voice, which says, 'I'm offering me, which is unique, very special, and incidentally whatever made you think that Source would ever feel let down by me?'

Just like the fear I had before releasing my first poem on Skyros, I now face the fear of releasing my first book. After all, I'm just an ordinary person, not regarded as being particularly well-educated academically, definitely not with a wide vocabulary, yet I have this desire to share what I know and reach out to others through my writing. When fear pops in on occasions like this, I remind myself of two things. The first is all the jobs I've applied for in my life. My stomach would churn before every interview, yet as soon as I was in there it always went away and I became free, alive, everything just flowed. I always loved the experience. I never went for a job I didn't want and I got every job I went for. The second is when, on one of my early visits to Findhorn, I took part in my first Transformation Game*. I was playing the game with two other people, and as the game was coming to a conclusion a message came to me as clearly as if it had been spoken by one of the group. It said, 'Being you is what serves me best.'

At the beginning of the game, I had asked how best I might serve. I suppose I was expecting a job title or something a little more directive, but these words were so empowering. I believe that when I hear messages like this from Source the message has gone out to all persons and is picked up by those who need to hear it. I was grateful to be listening at that time. To know that as long as I am awake, listening, communing, reflecting and walking my talk as congruently as I can, then it is the closest I am capable of being to my true self. Knowing that this is what serves my Source the best just fills me with love and gratitude and is the relationship I want to emulate with those around me. Working on identifying my own needs has helped me identify them in another. It is from that place that I can choose to meet another's need as if it were my own.

---

* A game of life devised at Findhorn and now facilitated and played by people throughout the world.

Remembering these two things is helping me move through my current fear. As a child, when faced with fear I did one of two things. I would either hide under the duvet or fight the fear. That remained a pattern for most of my life. I feel now that it no longer serves me. Fear always seemed to be hanging around in its different guises, which prevented me from connecting with my true self. I swung between being what I thought people wanted me to be and, in my rebellious times, definitely being what I thought they didn't want me to be. Never giving a thought to what I truly wanted to be. With my newly developed relationship with fear, I now choose to see it as an indicator of how close I am to my true path. It reminds me how much I respect what I'm doing and how much I must want to do it, if fear is turning up. When I face the fear, it allows me to be truthful with myself, and what that usually shows me is that I have the skills and talents within me or around me to move through the fear to the other side. I've also learnt that when I turn up for myself, so does God. Past experiences have shown me that once I've travelled through the void of fear, the beauty I discover is well worth the trip.

Creativity and communication are both challenges in my life, ones I am constantly working with. My school experiences were, shall we say, less than encouraging, and I chose to believe pretty early on that no matter how hard I tried it wasn't appreciated. Not surprisingly, after a while, I gave up. It appeared that I was much better understood verbally than I was by the written word. I know I would never have got into my grammar school had it not been for my interview. My written work would be handed back with several large red 'S's scrawled across the page and my heart would feel as if it had been pierced by tiny daggers. However, I loved school and learning and am a champion of lifelong learning. As a child, I was enthralled by all the wonders that were being shared with me by the teachers, the books and the assignments. Bit by bit, I shrivelled up and died inside when I saw the words 'Jacqueline can do better'. Didn't they know I was doing my best? Whenever I submitted my work to them, I felt as if it were a work of art and was expecting appreciation in return instead of the ridicule and humiliation I chose to feel. When my tactic of developing spidery handwriting to cover up the incorrect spelling came back with even worse comments, I gave up and wrote very little and obviously received other labels, such as 'lazy' or 'rebellious'.

Forty years later, on entering Ruskin College aged fifty, I discovered I was borderline dyslexic. I cried when I was told the news and was instantly offered counselling. Bless them. Didn't they realise that these were tears of joy and relief? All I wanted to do was hug myself and tell myself what a good job I had done over the years managing what I had without knowing this. In the jobs I'd held, I'd always preferred going for the meeting to submitting a written report. Sometimes the reports were necessary and they would cause me such pain to write. If I couldn't get out of writing one then you could bet your bottom dollar it would be produced at the eleventh hour, when nothing else was going to save me from doing it.

I have noticed resistance turning up on many occasions while I've been writing this book, but it wasn't from fear of writing. It was, I discovered, a fear of how I might be judged on my reasons for doing this. My ego would come up and say that I was just doing it to be famous, and that was presented as a negative motive. Ego was being very clever, as it was reminding me of the time I attended one of Barbara Winter's workshops, about four years ago, which was based on her book, *Making a Living Without a Job*. We were asked to go through a list of aims and tick those that were applicable to us. 'Being famous' was one among many that I ticked. It was quite a surprise for me to see that I had ticked that one. What I realised was that the reason was that I wanted the chance of connecting and sharing with more people, to have the opportunity to travel and to learn more. I see it as a spiral where I learn, I become, I share, I learn, I become, and so it continues.

I've witnessed many famous people doing great works, and Bob Geldof instantly comes to mind. As some of you may remember, Bob was very moved by the effects of the famine he saw in Africa and through his contacts with other famous musicians Band Aid was formed. Twenty years later, it is still remembered and the work started by him is continuing. Even if he hadn't been famous, I believe he would have been touched and motivated to do something about the situation, but I'm not sure that the relief or indeed the political impact would have been the same. I saw the same opportunities arise with Jamie Oliver and his passion for helping schoolchildren to eat more healthily. He also did it with *Fifteen*, where he wanted to help young people empower themselves through their culinary talents. So now, when my ego says, 'You're doing this to be famous', my response is 'I'd be grateful and willing to be able to serve in that way.'

OK, I admit there is a bit of an uncomfortable feeling about it, and so I ask the fear what its message is this time. For me, this is about sharing my story to illustrate the learning. I haven't always been as connected to my spiritual path as I am today, and I have done things in my life that I would have preferred to have done differently. Like many people, I'm sure, I wish I'd been a better daughter, sister, student, girlfriend, wife, mother, co-worker, manager, partner, grandmother. What keeps me centred around this is in believing that with the skills and knowledge I had I was operating at the best I could on the physical, mental, emotional and spiritual levels at any given time. The fact that I did not heal the wounds of my own childhood before I became a parent has caused me the most pain and tears. My attempts to form loving relationships were also painful; it was like being asked to create the Taj Mahal with nothing but rice paper. That I was so deep in my pain that I could try to take my life and abandon all those around me now seems so unimaginable.

Recently, I have looked back over my life with my new understandings of personal responsibility. With these new eyes I see only my actions, my choices, and through forgiveness and acceptance I am at peace with myself. It isn't that other people are irrelevant; it is just that the part they played is only relevant with regard to how I was triggered by or responded to it. It is from this place that I choose to live my life in the present, being in the moment, accepting and releasing the past and being joyful about my life every day. I am pleased to be able to say that I am fully present and willing to be in this body, on this earth, at this time, doing the work that is unfolding before me and being part of the relationships that surround me.

Another fear that I'm facing from producing a book based on my own experience is that I, my family and my friends are open to public scrutiny and appraisal. Do I have the right to do that? My answer now is 'yes', as long as I choose to take personal responsibility for my life – all of it – and not to use it as a tool to judge or blame others. When I first started writing this book while studying creative writing at Ruskin, I knew what I was writing could never published. Well, not the way it was written then. On reflection, I could see that the first draft was a vehicle for my own therapy. Albeit personally enlightening, it would not have been useful to anyone else. What I'd written was from the heart, but it was aimed externally and I could see a lot of blame and judgement of the roles other people had played throughout my journey. I think it can be quite useful to write in that way as part of a healing process, but not for publication. It felt so good to get my truth, as it was then, out. To get in touch with my feelings and to know what thoughts I was holding onto. But when I saw them on paper I realised that those thoughts and feelings were no longer true to me. The realisation that hit me was that I wouldn't want my children to read that book, and that will continue to be my litmus test for any work I offer up. I found it to be morbid and draining, which probably explains why it lay dormant during my time at Findhorn and in Croatia.

I now feel this book comes from a place of passion, where I take full responsibility for my life and the events and people I have attracted to me. I write it from a place of I, and I'm hoping that this shift is one that will empower others who are looking at their own journeys.

I get my inspiration in many ways, sometimes through songs, and one that caught my attention towards the end of 2005 when I was struggling with 'shall I, shan't I write and publish?' was 'That's My Goal' by Shayne Ward. He was the 2005 winner of the *X Factor*. Something had drawn me to the programme. It was strange, really, as I didn't have a television and had only seen parts of the series when visiting other people's houses. I was staying with a friend from my Ruskin days one weekend, and asked if she would mind watching the programme, as it was the final that evening. During the programme, the finalists sang the song that would be released by the winner. The words, the way Shayne sang them and the subsequent video release made my spine shiver. I could identify with all of it. It was relevant and very synchronistic that I was to hear that message when I was contemplating whether or not to publish my book. I was very sure I was meant to be watching this.

After Shayne's win, the press began releasing less-than-complimentary stories about his family. That reminded me of my fear of going public with my book. Let's face it: I have a family history that would be considered less than idyllic and we weren't always peaceful or able to keep together.

'Your journey has been worthless,' my fear was saying. 'You've spent most of your life being a warrior. You've had broken relations, your family is fragmented, and what sort of mother have you been? They will crucify you.'

Was I afraid to put my head above the parapet?

'Yes' was my initial response.

That was when I was judging myself, my family and maybe the people who would be reading this book. It was the line 'I'm not here to say I'm sorry' and the way I felt those words in my body that spoke so passionately to me. What I was feeling was that I'm not here to apologise for living the life I've led. I'm here to celebrate the life I'm living. It isn't about shrinking any more; it's about fullness and living as powerfully as I can.

My fear of the concept of power came from what I had previously witnessed. In this life it would have been from acts of 'power over', such as bullying, humiliation and abuse, physical, mental, emotional, financial, sexual and verbal. In previous life experiences, it would have been where the power of the light through ego transgressed and went into the dark: bringing about the decline of Atlantis, for example. Often power can be abused, and I think this is why, when I respect it so much, I fear what it might become. But I can't let that hold me back in this lifetime, as it keeps me small. All I can do is trust that I stay grounded, centred and in the light.

The words of Shayne's song also took me back to my attempted suicide and remembering that afterwards, not once did I feel ashamed of what I had done. Yes, I know there would have been two children without a mother, brothers without a sister and parents without a daughter, and so I can't explain why I didn't feel ashamed; I just felt different. I felt stronger. It was as if I had made a decision to be here. I could have gone, but I came back, and I think that takes courage and commitment. Afterwards, I made a decision to start again, and I knew 100 per cent that I wouldn't go down that route again. It was an inner knowing that I couldn't explain to anyone, not even myself. It was just the truth. I was a working mother, so after some time off to recuperate it was time to go back to work. I later heard that there was one person in the office who felt I should be too ashamed to go back. I couldn't understand what that was about. I'd been ill and now I was on the mend. To me, that was the beginning and the end of it. There are another couple of lines from Shayne's song that go: 'You know where I come from; you know my story.' I suppose for me what's important is who the 'I' that I share with the world is. When I face the real me through my eyes and through Source's eyes, there is an acceptance and a power from the living and being. It is my true self that allows my entire story to be accessed. I'm reminded of the Buddhist monk who would nod his head saying 'is that so?' regardless if the words spoken were complimentary or not. It is all of me that makes up the whole.

> I'm here to say I'm ready
> And I've finally thought it through.

These two lines sum up where I am right now. I feel ready, ready to know and celebrate my true self and to continually work on that process knowing that, as I do, so I grow closer to spirit. I'm also ready to work with others who want to share part of their journey with me.

> I'm not here to let your heart go,
> I'm not giving up, oh no,
> I'm here to win your heart and soul,
> That's my goal.

These few lines are an intention, a mantra to myself. There is no need to sing them to Spirit, because that heart has always been open to me.

So for me this experience was a 'wake-up' call. This was my cue to stop apologising for my life. Now is the time to accept it lovingly and to celebrate the growth and transformation because of it. I am ready to accept all the truths and have no need to hide anything. After all, when you eventually come clean and become naked in front of yourself, there is no need to lie to anyone else. I now know that I have always been naked before Source and loved for exactly who I am. For me, there are no secrets. Everything is known at an energetic level anyway, and that level reacts or responds to it regardless of whether we think it's a secret or not.

I said there were three things to do with Shayne's song that spoke to me and the last of these was the video recording that accompanied his debut single. For those of you who haven't watched it, it shows clips from the show and his journey through it from start to finish. For me, it encapsulates a lot of the feelings I've had on my journey: the determination, the joy, the relief, the excitement, the hope, the tears and the glory. Sometimes we shy away from words like 'glory' when referring to ourselves. Why do we do that, I wonder. I believe that when we have an understanding of our magnificence, our splendour, beauty, wonder and brilliance, we are more connected to our own Source and are more likely to connect with and witness the Source in another.

There was more to walking my talk than writing this book. There was another leap of faith to be made. This would come in the form of releasing all my physical securities again. I had very little savings left. I'm blessed that I had enough to support me over the last three years, but now I was faced with using the last I had to rent somewhere I could write for a few months and trusting that I would be able to sustain myself. The other option would be to stay where I was and maybe never write it.

For me, the time has come when my book needs to grow, to breathe, to have a life of its own. Just like giving birth or when my children reached adulthood, I now have to let my book go. That time is now. Other fears creep in when I'm not paying attention, like what will happen if I release the book and no one wants to publish it, or read it! However, those thoughts are quickly followed by: worse than that, what if I quit five minutes before a miracle happens? What if I don't put it forward for publication and my opportunity to share it is lost? For me, that is now the greater concern. I was inspired by Marianne Williamson, when in her book *A Return to Love* I read, 'Our deepest fear is not that we are inadequate. Our deepest fear is that we are powerful beyond measure.' Nick Williams, author of the book *Powerful Beyond Measure* writes, 'At the heart of each of us is a power beyond measure – the power of love and the power of creation. This is our true identity; it is who we are and how we were created. We can awaken from our dream of littleness into the truth of our spiritual greatness.' The sharing of their gifts and talents has enabled me to connect with my power, my passion, and creatively share it from my heart.

Facing up to realising my dream was one thing; creating groups to help people realise theirs was another; now I was going to publically be putting my faith in my inner guidance. The big question was: how was I going to move from a home I was living in rent- and bill-free – by working in exchange for it – and manifest a place where I could write and sustain myself until this book was written? 'One step at a time' was the message I got back. 'Taking baby steps,' Nick says. I needed to show the Universe that I was serious. This was the time and I meant it.

When I tuned in, I felt that I would need three months to put everything down on paper and dedicate myself every day to my new job of being a writer. I would need to be disciplined; I knew that. I can remember fighting against the word 'discipline' for many years. For me, it had always been a negative word. I had witnessed adults using it over children, not always fairly, I thought. I saw people use it through pulpits, soap boxes, prisons, and it often felt unjust. It wasn't until I had a discussion with a friend on my feelings about the word that I began to see that holding it solely in a negative light was not seeing the whole of it. Discipline was linked to being a disciple, so, for me, self-discipline meant being a disciple of oneself. That now seems something I can say 'yes' to. I wanted to be a disciple of my heart and soul and to work from a place of Source. I also needed to have a contract with myself; it would mean that I was to turn up for the job in hand and treat myself like anyone else I'd ever worked for. I believe I have a pretty exemplary record at being an employee and a manager, so I would now need to combine those talents and give myself my all.

I decided to attempt a visualisation to see where I'd be guided to write my book. I was shown a very large house: much larger than I could currently rent or own, but every time I thought about it the same picture would come to mind and I would take a virtual remote viewing around it. I didn't rule out winning the lottery or someone offering me a place like that to work from, but still I didn't seem to be attracting it. Not until much later did I realise that I was putting a box around my possibilities because I was thinking I needed to own this place. I wanted it to be large enough for me to live and work in, to write my book and allow space for another project I was working on, 'Inspirational Voices', to be birthed. I was happy to offer the house up to anyone else who wanted to live and work there. Yet still it didn't come. So, as my deadline for moving out of my accommodation came close, some friends offered me a room in their house. It was very generous of them, as they had only just moved into it themselves and I knew how precious it was to them. My girlfriend in particular had been a friend and supporter of mine for years. She had written testimonials for me as part of an entry requirement for both Ruskin and the Foundation Programme at Findhorn. We had originally met through work, become friends, gone clubbing together, shared our tears and laughter, gone on holiday with each other, but most of all we supported each other unconditionally. Regardless of whether we thought the other was doing the right thing or not, we never blamed, judged or criticised. We were always there for each other, and with her new partner she was there again.

I looked at all the accommodation adverts, but nothing jumped out of me. Before moving out of my studio flat in central Reading, I had seen an advert in a local holistic energy magazine that was advertising 'large bedroom, with en-suite sharing holistic house in Ashbury, Oxon, close to Swindon'. I tuned into it but got a 'no' at the time. Here I was a month later and it was calling me again. Well, a phone call wouldn't hurt, would it? The interesting thing was that there was another advert that day which drew my attention, and that was for shared accommodation just outside Reading. This place was well within my budget for a six-month contract, but it was advertised through an agent. My current freelance position was not attractive to them and I was declined a viewing even though my savings would cover a six-month contract. The Ashbury house on the other hand was way above budget; in fact, it would take the rest of my savings to afford it for three months. Despite that, I made an appointment to view and went down with a couple of girlfriends of mine about a week later. It was a lovely house and I decided that it would be great to write in. I suppose you might describe it as a 'posh commune'; alternatively, you could say it was a shared house for like-hearted people. I felt I wanted to put my cards on the table about not being able to afford a six-month contract. Fortunately for me, that didn't put them off. They offered me a three-month one if I wanted to come.

A few days later, I decided to go for a second visit with another friend of mine. I felt exactly the same as I had before. I had even picked out my bedroom, but there was something holding me back. It felt like about five per cent of me couldn't commit and I didn't know what that was about. So off I went again to mull it over. It would be some months later before I knew that one of the owners of the house had had some reluctance about the project at the time. Not much, I was told; maybe five per cent. I was beginning to realise that I was able to tune into more than I had previously acknowledged.

My fear for financial security was also coming up again and also my desire for some roots, a place I could call my home that wouldn't be under the threat of being taken away from me. It was time again to release my fear and walk through it. I asked myself this question:

'If money and owning your own property weren't the issues right now, would you choose this house to write and live in?'

The answer was a big '*yes*'.

Another visit was in order, but this time I knew I needed to go on my own. Each time I had been there before, I had wanted to go into the shop and the pub. I wanted to get a real feel for the community I was potentially going to belong to. It wasn't a large village and I wanted to feel part of it as well as part of the community within the house. A friend of mine lent me a car and I set off again. As I travelled down, it started to snow, which is always a happy sign for me as both my sons were born on snowy days. For me, it is a sign for birth, beauty and new beginnings. Just as I arrived in the village, I received a phone call from one of my friends who wanted to run an idea about a project she was involved in past me. There I was in what was potentially going to be my new community, and I could still be in contact with my friends and be part of their lives. That was another plus sign for me. I was also pleased to know that there was a good mobile phone reception, as I knew there wasn't yet a broadband connection. I went into the shop-cum-post office and saw two copies of *Spirit and Destiny* on the rack, and I felt that was another good sign. I was currently subscribing to the magazine and had had a letter published in there as a new reader. The woman behind the counter was friendly and I picked up a couple of local papers to take with me to the pub. The people I spoke to there were sociable, too. I explained I was thinking of moving into the village and they were happy to tell me it was a friendly place and I was bound to be welcomed. As I went back to pick up my car, the local bus was dropping off villagers who had been shopping. Even though they were laden with bags and it was snowing, they still smiled and passed the time of day. For me, it was a very positive experience. Before I even got to my appointment at the house, I'd made up my mind that I was going to take it.

Once I'd walked through the fear of lack of financial security, an idea came to me. As getting a commission for writing was usually out of the question for a new writer, what if I could attract some sponsorship? This would help me concentrate on the writing knowing that I could support myself for a few more months while sending out a book proposal and seeking a commission. I reminded myself that I was pretty good at manifesting things. In the past I had been quite a successful fundraiser for organisations I'd been involved with, and my scheme for equipping my studio flat when I came back from Croatia had worked perfectly. Maybe I could find some sponsorship, I thought. One text did it. The person I contacted offered to sponsor me for two months.

I made the phone call to the Ashbury landlords and moved into the house on 1 March 2006. I was now living in a place I felt was my home and I was a writer, group facilitator, coach, spiritual dreambuilder and community member. I also knew who I was in all of my relationships. I was loved and loving unconditionally, attaching no expectations and wanting nothing other than what was freely offered. I was beginning to notice that I was able to create a sense of home wherever I was. I felt like me, the Jacqueline Iris Daly I had been born to be. Why had I been hiding my light for so long?

As the days go by and my book begins to grow, I'm blessed with wonderful supportive friends, family and people like Nick Williams, who offered to appraise my work before I offered it up for publication. Nick and Barbara Winter have been great inspirators, as have William Bloom, Caroline Myss, Marianne Williamson, Franco Santoro, Eileen Caddy, Deepak Chopra, Diana Cooper, Doreen Virtue, James F. Twyman, Dr Brian Weiss, Louise L. Hay, Eckhart Tolle, Mother Teresa, Gordon Smith, Brandon Bays, Bob Geldof and Richard Branson. Not forgetting Pamela Stephenson and Billy Connelly, who indirectly inspired me to take to the stage for the first time in my life and release my poem 'Postcard to Myself'.

I've been passionate about injustice for most of my life and have tried in various ways to play my part. I remember at the time being surrounded by people who said, 'You can't make a difference. You are just one person.' I chose not to believe that on the surface, but underneath it was always me who held me back, not others as I may have previously thought. It was the lack of love for myself and my sense of unworthiness that hindered me. The 'hand-me-down' statement 'Jacqueline could do better' needed to be exorcised. It only served to reinforce that I was not good enough. It disempowered me and prevented me from seeing the beauty. It never allowed the spark in me to be fanned into the flame it is now. I have now chosen to reframe that statement and choose to become better. To expand, to grow and to become limitless. I choose to believe that the work I do is a gift to myself and the world. My own words told me that on Erraid and now I am feeling their truthfulness.

I knew there was a spark that twinkled inside of my
soul,
But now it's a flame burning brightly and some may
see its glow.
It may help to bring life to other sparks who are
searching for what they don't know,
And they too will become flames and others will then
see their glow.

Nothing I've said in this book is new. It doesn't belong to me, and my prayer is one of gratitude to those who have inspired me. I'm blessed that my life is full of joy, beauty and peace. I am surrounded by dreambuilders and peacemakers.

My soul has brought me to a beautiful place where all
in my heart seems right.
I choose to give myself complete; no longer afraid, I
don't fight.
So in celebration of today I dedicate myself to Fun,
And in the words of the Carpenters, 'I've only just
begun'.

***** Exercises *****

Time for review – are there any areas of your life where you wish you were more congruent? Where you were walking your talk more? What 'baby step' can you take today that will start to bring that back into alignment? What steps can you take over the next weeks and months?

What descriptions would you like after your name that identify who you are? Were there some that came to mind that you censored or were uncomfortable with? Why not take some time to explore the reasons for that? If there are areas in your life where you are acting small, in what ways can you become bolder?

Your relationship with Source – what words would you use to describe it? How do you distinguish the inner messages you get from that connection from those of your ego?

Your relationship with fear – what are your usual responses when faced with fear? How do you and those around you feed your fear? Do you recognise all of its guises? Is resistance one of the forms in which it presents itself to you? How many of the following do you recognise: 'I'll just tidy up first', 'I'll just fix myself a snack', 'when I can find more time' or 'when I've got a bit more energy'? Why not list the things you would currently like to do and the reasons you are using which might hold you back? Look back at each one and see how it feels to say that you are fearless and even excited about doing them. What help do you need to walk through each fear? Which ones are internal and ones you can deal with yourself? Which ones require additional information, skill or experience? What's aiding you and what's stopping you?

Have you noticed any messages coming through songs? If you need help and guidance with something at the moment, why not pay attention to the songs that come your way and see if there are any answers there for you? Have you noticed any other ways in which you often receive inspiration or guidance?

Are you saying 'yes' to being who you are right now, in the body you are in, alive at this moment in time, on this planet? If not, explore where the 'no's are and feel what changes need to take place to transform them into a 'yes'.

Expressing your true feelings – sometimes we are held back from speaking our truth, even to ourselves. Take this opportunity to see what truly wants to be expressed and to whom. Remember it isn't necessary to actually express it to the person who comes to mind. What is useful, however, is finding a way that works for you to express it. It can be written, spoken, drawn, danced or expressed in any other way that comes to you. The main thing is to express it and feel it. Once you do, you will usually find that a space is cleared for love to come in. Identify what your needs are around the issue and what you feel. If you do still need to convey your true feelings to a person/group/family, it is more powerful if you express them from a place of 'I', identifying what you feel and what your needs are without blame or judgement. (If you want to develop this way of communicating, I suggest you check out Marshall Rosenberg's *Nonviolent Communication*).

The Final Chapter

Except there Never really Is a Final Chapter

I HAD FELT MY BOOK WAS COMPLETE AND HAD EVEN POSTED off a proposal to Hays Publishing, hoping that my book among the many they received would be one of the ones to be published. That wasn't to be. Even though the answer was a 'no', I felt I was being held with even more gifts in the guise of insights coming my way. With the new-age technology, this new-age spirituality was transacted via email. After downloading their information on how to submit work to Hays, I received a friendly reply with clear information that my proposal had been received intact and that I could expect a response within about eight weeks.

At first I was surprised when I realised that I was more than happy to wait that amount of time. When I pondered why, I realised that it felt as if this book were my baby and it was now having its first outing. Feedback and comments on it could wait because as far as I was concerned it was absolutely perfect in its uniqueness, as were my own two sons when I gave birth to them. As the weeks passed by it seemed that I was the only person who was not counting the days. If I had had a pound for each time I was asked if there was any news of the book then I would certainly be well-off.

I suppose I wasn't so surprised by the interest my journey was attracting. I'd had such a tremendous amount of support from family, friends and clients for the writing and publication that I never actually felt I was doing it on my own. Which, of course, I wasn't, as I was sure I was being guided. I'd wondered about that at times. 'Being guided' can sound quite ostentatious, can't it? My trust in this was being tested. I would hear myself say, 'Surely if I were being guided then my book would be written more eloquently or with more esoteric information?' I would hear myself say that this was a very ordinary story, written by an ordinary person, in very ordinary language. No prizes for literary prose or the like. So why would it be guided in this style and through me?

'Exactly' was the response I received. 'Because you are you. And being you is what serves me best. The plan is that that this book is to be accessible to all who need to experience and identify with similar experiences to yours. Yes, the writing does have a childlike quality. That's a plus, you know. Often, the lives people are living are based on some crucial happenings they experienced as children, and it is their hurt or inner child that will respond to the experiences and exercises that are included in this offering. It is often at those times that people shut down their true selves and completely forget their purpose for being here. It's from this place that they will be awoken, and the words in this book offer up the best opportunity for them to remember their purpose and achieve it.

'Another reason is that we knew you would remember, even at a subconscious level, that you had said "yes" to this a very long time ago. Not only to writing this book, but to the next steps that you are becoming aware of. It took you a while, though, didn't it? Yet we were happy to wait because your unfolding was such a picture. Why would we want to change one stroke of the masterpiece? Once awoken, there was no stopping you. You were constantly alert, eagerly wanting to discover the real you at every bend and turn. You are a beacon of light and you have already drawn so many people to you by committing yourself to this adventure. Once you'd seen the book being published in your mind's eye and saw all the sparkles around it, you knew that one day it would be published. It was then that we knew you really did believe. All you had to do then was learn from this experience as much as you had from the writing. Hence we encouraged you to write this final chapter.

'You see, there never is a final chapter. Not to anything. Not even life. There are only ever new beginnings, new opportunities, new levels of awareness and experiences. Life is like a spiral. Everything comes around and goes around, yet when you arrive back at the beginning it looks new. That's because you are different and the people you are interacting with are different and even the environment is different. T S Elliot wrote, "We shall not cease from exploration. And the end of all our exploring will be to arrive where we started, and know the place for the first time."

'Do you remember how different you felt when you arrived back in Reading after leaving there to study in Oxford, then moving on to live in a community in Findhorn and then Croatia? You couldn't believe the changes in yourself, others and the town itself. You noticed all the different languages, particularly those from Eastern Europe. There were even shops dedicated to Polish produce and an edition of a local newspaper printed in that language. You enjoyed this new weave of peoples, languages, cultures, which added richness to the tapestry of life in Reading. And then there were the new friends, acquaintances and groups you were attracted to and whom you attracted. You wondered where all these people had been when you lived there three years previously. At first it was just a dozen or so, and then they grew around you until they became a community living within a community and whose numbers were too many to count.

'Then, of course, there was the recurrence of lessons, experiences that you thought you had "dealt with". At first you felt disappointed. However, you began to understand that as you grew to a new level so you needed to address some of these lessons again there. By now you knew you had choices which included how quickly, gracefully and insightfully you wanted to process these lessons. You also knew that what you wanted might not match what you needed. Yet your prayers were constantly being answered. When they weren't in the way you had thought, you instantly knew that you had attached an expectation of outcome to that request. You had reached new levels of acceptance and detachment, which aided not only your processing but your being. You also knew that for some of those lessons this was the last learning. You had cleared the karma on that particular issue. You had reached the stage where you could safely say that you had seen it, done it and worn the T-shirt. So, although not an ending or a final chapter, there was a sense of completion. There was an opportunity to enter the void once more and await a new beginning, a new opportunity.

'So, my little one, it's time for this book to continue its journey. We will guide you each step of the way, as we know you are willing to continue working with us. Yes, of course. You are wondering who we are. We, like you, are the disciples of the Christ energy. We channel through you the unconditional love and healing from the eternal Father, through his eternal son. It will be through the telling of your story, the sharing of your experiences, the passion of your sense of oneness, of community, unity and peace that you will be able to connect with others and help lead them home.'

In some ways, seeing those words above is a bit of a surprise, yet they flowed through me just as any of the others I've written or the previously shorter messages I have received. I believe what is most important for me now is how I work with them. For me, that means taking them into the silence and reviewing their meaning from my highest self, my soul's energy. I do this so that I may scrutinise the message and put it through my 'litmus test'. I examine any resistances and check for the presence of ego. Then, if I believe that the message comes via my higher self, I find my own understanding of what that means to me and then integrate its essence into my 'beingness'. From that place, I own the words and can again stand in my power by taking personal responsibility for my understanding and any future words, thoughts and deeds. I don't hide behind it by saying 'My guidance says I must do this' or 'I'm only following my guidance'.

I believe there are no idols on the earth plane or anywhere else. There are certainly people, places and experiences that will shine a light on an issue for me. Many, many times in my life I have been and will continue to be grateful for such insights. Yet the real beauty for me comes from letting my higher self play the game of life. It has, unknown to me, been there as a constant guide from the very beginning. Having waited patiently as a 'sub' on the football bench, it now takes its rightful place and helps me play the game of my life. It's one of the most empowering things I've done. I've now learnt to trust myself, to be grateful to myself, to be at peace with myself and to see the beauty in myself. What I see in the mirror of life now is beauty. My deepest and most humbling experience was to accept that what I was seeing was *me*.

The other gift was in understanding that, although I had ended each day with prayers of gratitude, I had previously forgotten to add my name. Until now, that is. I am very grateful for being *me*.

I believe in the inner and outer divinity, which means to me that I AM. In a way, this empowers me to be my own creator in the game called life. I try my best to come from a place I refer to as my higher self. And I'm not convinced that the Christ energy is solely for Christians. I am very moved to find references to God and Christ in the *Autobiography of a Yogi* by Paramahansan Yogananda, written in 1946. Yogananda is one among many who inspire me. Yogananda popularised yoga and meditation in the west and his books and teachings emphasise the oneness of all spiritual and religious paths with a focus on developing a deep love connection with the oneness, which from my experience is often called by many different names. I have certainly discovered that through the practice of Kriya Yoga, mentioned in Yogananda's book, my life has been richly enhanced. Kriya's legacy was passed on to Yogananda from his guru, Sri Yukleswar, and to him via the teachings of Babaji. In his book, Yogananda refers to Babaji as a *maha avatara*, or a great avatar. *Avatara* is a Sanskrit word which means 'descent' or incarnation of the Godhead in human form.

Kriya yoga opens me up and encourages flexibility on all levels. Until this point I had not practiced yoga before, except for two classes over twenty years ago. During and after my first Kriya class, I had such profound experiences. In some ways it's hard to explain my experience in words, but I will give it my best shot. Although I was listening and following the instructions of the teacher, I was also aware of being in a very meditative state, sensing the essences of peace and love. At times I also felt I had been regressed in time and could feel myself living a very different life in India. Amazing, really, because India was always one of the places I avoided visiting on my travels. During the class and regression, I could actually smell the spices that lay in woven baskets in front of me. I was able to see the rich colours of the spices and the environment with new eyes. This place was where I had experienced such love and peace – sitting in the dirt, offering my spices to those who wished to purchase them. The spices, it seemed, were just a by-product. The most profound experiences came from the interactions with the travellers who, taking a break from their journeys, sat with me and talked while sharing a cool drink of water from the well I tended. The exercises carried out during the class seemed to access all the corners I'd previously missed. This really was the equivalent of a good spring clean. It allowed things that I had invited up to surface and, once processed, to allow space for more light and love to fill.

I have felt similar experiences with the use of Reiki – an energy healing practice that was rediscovered by Dr Mikao Usui (1856–1926) after years of research. Hawayo Takata, an early Reiki Master and the first female and non-mainland Japanese Reiki Master, introduced Reiki to the west from her homeland of Hawaii. In Diane Stein's book, *Essential Reiki*, Takata is quoted as saying, 'I believe there exists one Supreme Being – the Absolute Infinite – a dynamic Force that governs the world and the universe. It is an unseen spiritual power that vibrates and all other powers fade into insignificance beside it. So, therefore, it is absolute! I shall call it Reiki because I studied under that expression. Being a universal force from the Great Divine Spirit, it belongs to all who seek and desire to learn the art of healing.' I feel blessed to have become a Reiki Master/Teacher and to be able to pass those teachings onto others.

Other blessings that I'm grateful for are my new-found experiences with my biological family and with current relationships. I thank everyone for waiting so long for me to return to my true self so that I could see their beauty. Only yesterday, I had the most loving of conversations with my mother. Thank you, Mum, for being you and holding the space for me to find myself. The same goes for my brother, whom I spoke to today. From my perspective, we too had a wonderful conversation, and I'm so grateful that a veil has been lifted from my eyes to allow me to see the beauty that has always been there. Thankfully for both of us, I no longer ask him to act as my judge.

I sometimes have this fantasy that we are all actors in a play. We have all agreed to the roles we are to act out and the lines we are to speak. At the end of the night, we take off the costumes and put on our ordinary clothes and return to ourselves. Our true selves. We return to love. Wasn't it Shakespeare who said 'All the world's a stage, and all the men and women merely players'? So it is with the deepest gratitude I thank all the supporting cast who have appeared with me in many, many performances of 'Awakening My True Self'.

Holding a space for another's healing is one of the truest expressions of love for me. I'm blessed to have a very, very dear friend from my Findhorn days who has over the years, week in, week out, worked with me on holding a space. At first, when we met at Findhorn, we were part of a spiritual support group with one other person. We met every week to meditate together and share from a soul place. We did not give verbal feedback unless invited and would unconditionally hold a space for each other. We released ourselves from judgement, criticism and advice, instead giving way to another. From here we were able to express, hear, feel and discover for ourselves all that needed to be heard. True, we may have felt triggers from another's sharing and sometimes experienced the most profound essence of love, yet we had agreed to hold that in the moment, in the oneness, so that we might all heal. Fortunately for me, after coming back from my travels I was able to link up again with one of my spiritual support group members and we – he in Scotland and I in either England or Wales – would share weekly on the phone. We continue holding a 'soul' place for each other. I know from what we have shared in what we call our 'free-fall' sessions at the end of our sharing – I guess others might call that chatting – our lives are richer and more healed from our commitment to turn up for each other from a place of love, to help each other heal. It has played an important part in my spiritual growth, and I'm discovering community and unity within myself and with others around me.

Blessed be.

It was a while ago we made this pact
I had nearly forgotten myself
But fortunately you remembered
And your message landed on my shelf
'Can I call you?' you enquired

And the memories came flooding back
We had agreed to meet up for healing
We remembered abundance, not lack
The words seemed to spill from the heart
And were heard from that place too
We remembered to remember who we are
And the memories came flooding through
We are both teachers and students, you see
Of the game that on this planet is called life
We had struggled with pain, found compassion
We embraced joy and released strife
We are mindful of being, not doing
Being present for each other's actions and words
With a growing sensation of freedom
We are soaring and flying like birds
There is no box to fit in
Or a label to describe what it is
The freedom we have from expectations
Allows us to be all that there is
'We are love,' we scream from the cliff top
And the wind she carries it away
To far-distant shores of remembrance
To release others from being slaves
So an awakening is stirring for all
And we have remembered to play our part
We choose always to be mindful
And to speak and listen from the heart
It is with gratitude I send love
On discovering these new laws
For remembering to remember to call
So that we can let love open all doors.

So at this point in time I do have peace in my world, in my relationships, and from this place I know it will ripple out. Again, reflecting the essence of a very wise teacher, Mother Teresa, it may be just one drop in the ocean, but it is one more drop. It is from this place that another inspirational woman's words come to mind – Eileen Caddy: 'All is very, very well.'

And so the story and healing of this soul continues. Like many actors, I'm currently resting, awaiting the next script. My higher self is my agent.

Blessings on your journey.

Chronology

- ⋆ 1952, 27 June 0.45 a.m. born Jacqueline Iris Daly – Farnham Common, Bucks.
- ⋆ 1956 attended St Mary's (Roman Catholic) School, Maidenhead
- ⋆ 1963 attended Maidenhead High School for Girls
- ⋆ 1968 attended part-time Berkshire College & part-time school – Commerce & Secretarial Course
- ⋆ 1970 left home, got engaged and married
- ⋆ 1973 moved to Plymouth
- ⋆ 1976 miscarriage of my daughter
- ⋆ 1978 first son born
- ⋆ 1982 second son born and three months later I was separated from the father of my children
- ⋆ 1983 divorced and moved to Reading, Berkshire
- ⋆ 1990 second marriage and attempted suicide
- ⋆ 1991 my elder son went to live with his father and step-mother in the West Country
- ⋆ 1992 divorced for second time
- ⋆ 1993 elder son temporarily returned home
- ⋆ 2000 split from long-term partner
- ⋆ New Year's Eve, 2001 heard God speak the word 'community' to me.
- ⋆ 2002 Queen Mother's Birthday – realisation that I might possibly have more life to live than I had so far

Jan – received first flyer advertising Women's Studies at Ruskin College, Oxford

Feb – received second Ruskin flyer, attended Ruskin Open Day

Apr – interview for Ruskin

Jun – aged fifty, beginning to realise the essence of there being a 'True Self'

Aug – went to Skyros – wrote first poem

Sept – became a student at Ruskin College, Oxford

Dec – first visit to the Findhorn Foundation – Experience Week Programme

★ 2003 passed exam at Ruskin with Distinction

Feb – second visit to Findhorn – Exploring Community Life programme

March–April – third Visit to Findhorn – Living in the Community Guest programme (LCG)

July – finished studies at Ruskin

July–Aug – nomad

Aug–Sept – fourth visit to Findhorn Foundation and second month of LCG

Sept – Fifth visit to Findhorn Foundation – Foundation Programme

Nov–Dec – week on Erraid

Dec–Jan – visited Colorado

★ 2004

Jan–June – Findhorn Foundation Community Member

June–Sept – working and living in Croatia

Sept–Dec – living in and transforming friend's house in Woodley, Reading

★ 2005 living in Reading

★ 2006 moved to Ashbury, Oxon

- ⋆ 2007 moved to Swansea, South Wales
- ⋆ 2009 publication of my first book – *Awakening the True Self*

Bibliography

Chopra, Deepak M.D., *Overcoming Addictions*, First Three Rivers Press, New York, 1997

Caddy, Eileen, *God Spoke to Me*, Findhorn Press, Scotland, 1992

Coelho, Paulo, *The Alchemist*, HarperCollins, London, 1993

Emoto, Dr Masaru, *The Hidden Messages of Water*, Simon & Schuster, New York, 2005

Emoto, Dr Masaru, *The True Power of Water*, Simon & Schuster, New York, 2005

Rosenberg, Marshal, *Non violent Communication*, IPG (PuddleDancer Press), Encinitas, 2003

Stein, Diane, *Essential Reiki*, Crossing Press, California, 1995

Stephenson, Pamela, *Billy*, HarperCollins, London, 2001

Tolle, Eckhart, *The Power of Now*, Hodder and Stoughton, London, 1999

Williamson, Marianne, *A Return to Love*, HarperCollins, London, 1992

Williamson, Marianne, *Illuminata – A Return to Prayer*, Rivermead Trade, 1999

Williams, Nick, *Powerful Beyond Measure*, (Bantam Edition) Transworld Publishers, London, 2004

Williams, Nick, *The Work We Were Born to Do*, Element, London, 1999

Yogananda, Paramahansan, *Autobiography of a Yogi*, Self-Realization Fellowship, California, 1978

Information and Contact Points

Ruskin College: www.ruskin.ac.uk

Findhorn Foundation: www.findhorn.org

Isle of Erraid: www.erraid.fslife.co.uk

Eileen Caddy: *Opening the Doors Within*

Louise Hay: www.louisehay.com

Transformation Game:
www.findhorn.org/tools/game/overview.html

Energies in Action: www.energiesinaction.co.uk

Nick Williams: www.nick-williams.com

Marianne Williamson: www.marianne.com

Paramahansa Yogananda: www.yogananda-srf.org

Kriya Yoga: www.kriya.org

Diana Cooper: www.dianacooper.com

Doreen Virtue: www.angeltherapy.com

Crystal & Indigo Children:
www.thecrystalchildren.com/crystal

Franco Santoro: www.astroshamanism.org

William Bloom: www.williambloom.com

The Waterboys: www.mikescottwaterboys.com

Dr Usui and Reiki: www.reiki.org

Atsitsa on the Greek Island of Skyros: www.skyros.co.uk

Dr Masaru Emoto – Hidden Messages of Water:
www.masaru-emoto.net

Chris James: www.chrisjames.net

Paulo Coelho: www.paulocoelho.com

Barbara Winter: www.barbarawinter.com

Caroline Myss: www.myss.com

Deepak Chopra: www.chopra.com

James F Twyman: www.emissaryoflight.com

Dr Brian Weiss: www.brianweiss.com

Eckhart Tolle: www.eckharttolle.com

Mother Teresa: www.motherteresa.org

Amma: www.amma.org

Gordon Smith: www.thepsychicbarber.co.uk

Brandon Bays: www.thejourney.com

Bob Geldof: www.bobgeldof.info

Pamela Stephenson & Billy Connelly: www.billyconnolly.com

The X Factor 2005–2007: www.xfactor.tv

Spirit and Destiny: www.bauer.co.uk

Mike Dooley: www.tut.com

Pluscarden Abbey: www.pluscardenabbey.org

Neale Donald Walsch: www.conversationswithgod.org

Jacqueline Daly: www.inspirationalvoicesswansea.co.uk;
www.energiesinaction.co.uk/JacquelineDalyWorkshops;
jacquelineirisdaly@hotmail.com

Printed in the United Kingdom by
Lightning Source UK Ltd., Milton Keynes
138576UK00001B/3/P

9 781847 483614